D0426680

CALGARY PUBLIC LIBRARY

NOV   2017

SIDE HUSTLE

ALSO BY CHRIS GUILLEBEAU

The Art of Non-Conformity
The $100 Startup
The Happiness of Pursuit
Born for This

SIDE HUSTLE

FROM IDEA TO INCOME IN 27 DAYS

CHRIS GUILLEBEAU

CROWN
BUSINESS
NEW YORK

Copyright © 2017 by Chris Guillebeau

All rights reserved.
Published in the United States by Crown Business,
an imprint of the Crown Publishing Group,
a division of Penguin Random House LLC, New York.
crownbusiness.com

CROWN BUSINESS is a trademark and CROWN and
the Rising Sun colophon are registered trademarks of
Penguin Random House LLC.

Crown Business books are available at special discounts
for bulk purchases for sales promotions or corporate use.
Special editions, including personalized covers,
excerpts of existing books, or books with corporate logos,
can be created in large quantities for special needs.
For more information, contact Premium Sales at (212) 572-2232
or email specialmarkets@penguinrandomhouse.com.

Library of Congress Cataloging-in-Publication data is available upon request.

Hardcover ISBN 978-1-5247-5884-4
Ebook ISBN 978-1-5247-5885-1
International Edition ISBN 978-1-5247-6243-8

PRINTED IN THE UNITED STATES OF AMERICA

Book design by Andrea Lau
Illustrations by Peter Arkle
Jacket design by Evan Gaffney and Tal Goretsky
Jacket photographs: (motorcycle side car) dpa picture alliance/Alamy Stock
Photo; (money bag) t.kimura/E+/Getty Images

10 9 8 7 6 5 4 3 2 1

First Edition

CONTENTS

YOUR 27-DAY PLAN

WEEK 1: BUILD AN ARSENAL OF IDEAS

A side hustle has many benefits, but it all starts with the right idea. This first week of hustling will teach you how to generate hustle ideas that actually work.

DAY 1. PREDICT THE FUTURE

The path from idea to income begins with your answer to an important question: Twenty-seven days from now, what will be different about your life?

DAY 2. LEARN HOW MONEY GROWS ON TREES

Some hustle ideas are better than others. Learn the three qualities of a great idea and how to find ones with the most potential.

DAY 3. BRAINSTORM, BORROW, OR STEAL IDEAS

Using what you've learned about high-potential ideas, brainstorm, borrow, or steal at least three possibilities for your hustle.

DAY 4. WEIGH THE OBSTACLES AND OPPORTUNITIES OF EACH IDEA

Now that you have several ideas, examine them more closely to understand their pros and cons.

DAY 5. FORECAST YOUR PROFIT ON THE BACK OF A NAPKIN

To estimate the profit of your side hustle, you don't need a finance degree or a scientific calculator. You just need a napkin, a pen, and the power of observation.

WEEK 2: SELECT YOUR BEST IDEA

Once you have multiple ideas, you need to be able to identify the best ones. Learn how to instantly rank and compare ideas so that you'll have confidence to proceed with the highest possible odds of success.

DAY 6. USE THE SIDE HUSTLE SELECTOR TO COMPARE IDEAS

Once you start thinking about side hustles, the ideas don't stop. This tool will show you how to apply "Tinder for Hustling" logic to pick the best one at any given time.

DAY 7. BECOME A DETECTIVE

As you move forward with an idea, study what other people are doing. Then, do it better or do it differently.

DAY 8. HAVE IMAGINARY COFFEE WITH YOUR IDEAL CUSTOMER

There's one person out there who meets your profile as the perfect customer. What can you learn from them?

DAY 9. TRANSFORM YOUR IDEA INTO AN OFFER

Once you have a great idea and a specific idea of who it's for, you need to transform that idea into an offer. An offer includes a promise, a pitch, and a price.

DAY 10. CREATE YOUR ORIGINS STORY

Like a comic book superhero, your side hustle needs a history. Don't just give 'em the facts; tell them a story.

WEEK 3: PREPARE FOR LIFTOFF

You've settled on your idea, you've transformed it into an offer, and you know who your ideal customer is. This week you'll learn how to help that person understand why they can't live without your offer, without getting bogged down in unimportant details.

DAY 11. ASSEMBLE THE NUTS AND BOLTS

Resourcefulness is your most valuable hustle skill. Get all the logistics out of the way so you can focus on more important things.

DAY 12. DECIDE HOW TO PRICE YOUR OFFER

Pricing can be a challenge even for experienced hustlers. Use the cost-plus model and follow two easy guidelines for much higher odds of success.

DAY 13. CREATE A SIDE HUSTLE SHOPPING LIST

Your hustle will require specific tools, resources, and deliverables. Learn to find, gather, or create everything you'll need to bring your offer into the world.

DAY 14. SET UP A WAY TO GET PAID

You've got a lot more than just an idea now—you're well under way to a real-life side hustle. Before proceeding, make sure you've also got a real-life way to get paid for it.

DAY 15. DESIGN YOUR FIRST WORKFLOW

You're almost to launch week. By listing out your next steps in an ordered fashion, you'll prevent mishaps and feel more confident.

BONUS STEP

DAY 16. SPEND 10 PERCENT MORE TIME ON THE MOST IMPORTANT TASKS

Many new hustlers get caught up in mundane details. Avoid that trap from the beginning, and keep your focus on just two things.

WEEK 4: LAUNCH YOUR IDEA TO THE RIGHT PEOPLE

After careful planning, you're all set to take your offer into the world. The time is now! Learn everything you need to know about marketing, testing, and showing up to the battlefield in a tank.

DAY 17. PUBLISH YOUR OFFER!

When's the best time to get your offer out in the world and see what happens? Usually before you feel totally confident.

DAY 18. SELL LIKE A GIRL SCOUT

Even with a great product or service, and a great offer to make your pitch, magic money doesn't usually fall from the sky. Channel your inner Girl Scout and make some sales!

DAY 19. ASK TEN PEOPLE FOR HELP

No man is an island, and few side hustles thrive without the help of friends and supporters. As you begin hustling, don't hesitate to ask friends, family, and maybe even your mail carrier to join your cause.

DAY 20. TEST, TEST, AND TEST AGAIN

When you're beginning a new hustle, you don't usually know which approach will be the most effective. To find out, try different things and keep a record of results.

DAY 21. BURN DOWN THE FURNITURE STORE

There's a very good reason why most of us will go out of our way to buy something that's on sale. Master the benefits of deals, discounts, and special offers—then put them to work for you.

BONUS STEP

DAY 22. FRAME YOUR FIRST DOLLAR

Take time to celebrate your initial achievements. There's more work to be done, but small victories can be disproportionately satisfying.

WEEK 5: REGROUP AND REFINE

Your hustle is out in the world! Congratulations—now let's see what you can do to raise the game.

DAY 23. TRACK YOUR PROGRESS AND DECIDE ON NEXT STEPS

As you learn more about the response to your hustle, take note of the most crucial metrics—then take action on what you learn.

DAY 24. GROW WHAT WORKS, LET GO OF WHAT DOESN'T

As your hustle grows, there are countless options to expand. Don't get distracted—identify what's working and do more of that.

DAY 25. LOOK FOR MONEY LYING UNDER A ROCK

If everything's going well, consider adding another version of it to better serve your customers. After all, if you saw a million dollars on the side of the road, wouldn't you pick it up?

DAY 26. GET IT OUT OF YOUR HEAD

Every hustle has key systems. Yours are probably stored in your head—and that's not always wise. To make significant improvements (and save more time) as you expand your hustle, systemize wherever you can.

DAY 27. BACK TO THE FUTURE

You've come to the end of the road . . . or is it the beginning? Decide whether to part ways with your first idea and try something else, keep growing it, or simply turn it into an ongoing source of income.

KITCHEN SINK

APPENDIX 1: SIDE HUSTLE STARTER KITS

APPENDIX 2: HOW TO VALIDATE AN IDEA WITH $10 AND A
              FACEBOOK ACCOUNT

APPENDIX 3: WRITE A LETTER TO YOUR IDEAL CUSTOMER

APPENDIX 4: BUY A RENTAL PROPERTY WITH A $1,575 DOWN
              PAYMENT

RESOURCES AND FREE STUFF

THE WAY OF THE HUSTLE

When a British man who managed a construction company wrote a series of fish tank reviews for an obscure website, he included links to several Amazon product listings at the end of the reviews. He knew he'd earn a small commission if visitors clicked through from the reviews and made a purchase, but he was so busy with his day job that after he posted the reviews, he promptly forgot about the whole thing. A few weeks later, a check arrived in the mail . . . for $350. His partner didn't believe it was real money until he took her out to a nice dinner with the proceeds.

At the time, he had no idea that this small project, created in a weekend, would go on to make hundreds of dollars. He also didn't know that *several years later* those same reviews would still be earning him an average of $700 a month, without any further work on his part. It wasn't retirement money, but it sure was nice.

Similarly, when a San Diego government employee offered to photograph a friend's wedding, he didn't know it would lead to an extra $3,500 every month. This employee didn't want to be a full-time wedding photographer, but the option to shoot an occasional wedding whenever he wants provides him with security and savings. He takes the jobs that accommodate his schedule and turns down the ones that don't, all while continuing to receive a steady paycheck from his "real" job.

When a Pennsylvania oil and gas sales rep started posting images on Pinterest, she wasn't a celebrity and didn't have a "revenue model." In addition to the day job, she was also a mom and a yoga teacher and active in her local community. Within a month, she had earned more than $1,000—much to her shock and happy surprise. After three years, she'd taken in more than $40,000, all while uploading photos whenever she had a break from her busy day.

These stories, all true, represent the way of the side hustle: defined as a moneymaking project you start on the side, usually while still working a day job. In other words, it's a way to create additional income without taking on the risks of going full throttle into the world of working for yourself.

Sure, for some people the thought of quitting their day job and striking out on their own is exhilarating. For many others, however, it can be terrifying. After all, whether or not you have a family to support or a mortgage to pay, a job that produces a steady income and provides health insurance is difficult, if not impossible, to give up.

But what if you could get a profitable idea off the ground with just a minimal investment of time, money, and effort—and you could make that happen *alongside* your stable and steady job? This book shows you how to do exactly that, with a step-by-step guide that takes you from idea to implementation in just twenty-seven days. The guide is designed for the busy and impatient. It's a detailed road map that will allow you to brainstorm, select, launch, and make money in under a month.

But a side hustle isn't *just* about putting extra cash in your pocket. In today's environment, where the idea of a business having any sense of loyalty to its workers has all but disappeared, the side hustle is the new job security. It affords you the ability to decide. When you receive multiple paychecks from different sources, you are no longer dependent on the whims of a single employer.

More income means more options. More options mean more freedom.

In the pages ahead you'll read many more stories like the ones mentioned above. Entertaining as they are, they also have a greater purpose. They're here to show you that *anyone* can build a fast track to freedom by increasing their income—using the skills they already have. No matter what it is you do in your day job, or whether you want to identify as an "entrepreneur" or not, you need a side hustle. If you follow this plan, you'll have one in less than a month.

What will your story be?

THE MONEY TREE

Did you ever hear the saying that money doesn't grow on trees? Parents sometimes say this to their kids when the kids want to buy everything in sight. These parents are only half right. Money *does* grow on trees—you just have to plant the right seeds, in the right soil. In each short chapter of this book, you'll read a story of someone who found a money tree and made it blossom—simply by putting an idea into action. Along the way, you'll learn how to uncover and unlock a replicable process you can tailor to your own hustle.

I hope you find these stories inspiring, but more than that I hope they inspire you to take action. There's a money tree out there waiting for you, too. In the next twenty-seven days, you'll learn how to find and nurture it, and then watch it grow.

Whether you're no stranger to side hustles or you're brand-new to the concept, this book will help you get up and running with a profitable project in a short period of time. All the details are in the next 250 pages, but here's what you need to know right now:

1. Everyone should have a side hustle. Even if you love your job, having more than one source of income will give you more freedom and more options.

2. It's not that hard to start one. You can do so in less than a month by following the lessons in this book.

3. To be successful at hustling, you first need to understand how to generate profitable ideas and then choose which one is best at any particular time. You'll learn both of these skills in the first half of the book.

4. Side hustles are all about action! You need to launch your idea, usually before you feel totally ready, then regroup and refine after seeing the initial results. You'll learn how to do this in the second half of the book.

WHAT YOU NEED AND WHAT YOU DON'T

There are very few prerequisites to side hustling. To be successful in using this model, mostly you need:

- **The right frame of mind.**
  Specifically, you need a willingness to learn *and* experiment. Even if you're a longtime serial hustler, some of what you'll learn here will be new to you. To get the most out of these lessons, you'll need to be willing to open your mind to a different way of thinking.

- **The willingness to act.**
  Even though I've tried to write a very practical book, merely reading it won't do much for you. You must be willing to follow the instructions and attempt the exercises. Modifying them is fine—they have to work for you—but if you want to be successful, you can't skip them entirely.

As you can see, the list of prerequisites is pretty basic. The list of what you *do not* need is far longer. This is important, because many people think that the ability to earn money outside of their day job is out of their reach. Luckily, these people are wrong. Let's get this out of the way right from the start:

- **You don't need much money.**

  Put away your credit cards (at least the ones with high limits) and don't worry about needing to raise capital or ask someone for a loan. The process I'll show you in the days ahead, along with the vast majority of ideas and stories you'll read about, do not require a large amount of money—and in some cases, no money at all is required.

- **You don't need much time.**

  To be fair, you'll need *some* time. But the time required to start a hustle should be minimal. The twenty-seven-day plan is designed to be doable alongside your existing commitments and take no more than one hour a day. If you want to work faster, or build your project to a higher level right away, that's fine and you can spend more time doing so—but you won't *have* to.

- **You don't need a business degree, or any kind of specialized education.**

  Most business education teaches people how to be a corporate manager, which is fine if that's what you do for your day job. But with a side hustle, you're starting your own business, not running someone else's. You don't need an MBA. You won't have to use complicated software or spreadsheets. Your financial forecasts can be written on the back of a napkin—and in fact, that's exactly what you'll learn to do on Day 5.

- **You don't need employees, assistants, or business partners.**
  You may want to get help at some point, but not right away. The initial goal is to start on your own, using your own skills and effort.

- **You don't need experience starting a business.**
  You don't need to be an "entrepreneur" to start a side hustle. Even if you have zero experience working for yourself, with the advice in this book and a little resourcefulness of your own, you'll have no problem taking your hustle from idea to profit.

In fact, some of these things (the money, the abundance of free time, even education) can actually be *detrimental* to your plan. If you have money to spend, you'll spend it. If you have an abundance of free time to waste, you'll waste it. Whatever you learned about business in school can sidetrack or prevent you from taking the simple steps you need to turn your idea into action. Last, at some point it may be wise to expand your team, but when you have to do everything yourself, you'll have to stick to what's essential. This plan will show you how.

WHY I WROTE THIS BOOK

I've been starting and operating side hustles my entire adult life. In fact, it's the only occupational path I've ever known. For more than twenty years, I've made a good living doing everything from importing coffee to building websites. Somewhere in that time, I also spent several years as an aid worker in West Africa, then pursued (and finished) a quest to visit every country in the world. If you asked me how to be a better employee, I wouldn't know what to tell you. But if you want to know how to create a new source of income, I can guide you each step of the way.

You can learn the way of the hustle, too. Once you acquire the skill of idea generation, you'll have no problem coming up with ideas whenever you need. Then, when you master the skill of making ideas happen, you'll be able to convert those ideas into income-producing assets.

It's like alchemy, except it's not magical. It's practical.

The sole purpose of this book is to help you increase your income *and* your security, giving you more options and allowing you to do more of what you want. If you accept this mission and commit to seeing it through, I promise to do everything I can to support you along the way.

HOW TO USE THE 27-DAY PLAN

Side hustle skills are not taught in school. Unless you were especially fortunate, you probably didn't learn them from your parents, either. There's nothing wrong with classroom knowledge, but it won't help you much here. The only way to master side hustle skills is by *doing*.

The other day I talked with someone who was in the process of starting her first hustle. She's a classic example of whom this book is written for. She has a good job and doesn't necessarily want to strike off on her own—but she also wanted to build something for herself outside her daytime work hours. In this case, her idea was to create a pop-up art show to sell her illustrations. Since she didn't know much about starting a business, she pursued what seemed like a normal course of action and signed up for an eight-week entrepreneurship class at a local college. Unfortunately, the class led mostly to frustration. "About 15 percent of what I learned was helpful," she told me. "But the rest was about things that were either mostly or completely irrelevant to my goals."

Consider this book to be a different kind of school. Instead of teaching you to write lengthy business plans and borrow money, it will show you a complete process of planning and action, condensed into a twenty-seven-day timeline.

And instead of showing up for class at a prescribed hour every day, you can learn these lessons on your own schedule, and on your own time. Nevertheless, you'll want to follow the general outline below, which shows how all the steps build together to bring you to a profitable hustle.

Each week focuses on a theme and is divided into five steps, with bonus steps in Weeks 3 and 4. Don't get hung up over how long any particular step takes you—some can be quickly completed, and some may take you longer than an actual day. The key point is to move through these stages in sequence.

Here are the objectives for each week:

WEEK 1: Learn to generate profitable ideas
WEEK 2: Select your best idea (not all ideas are created equal!)
WEEK 3: Prepare to share your best idea with the right group
of people
WEEK 4: Launch—probably before you're ready—and track
your results
WEEK 5: Regroup and refine

WEEK 1: BUILD AN ARSENAL OF IDEAS

Day 1:   Predict the Future

Day 2:   Learn How Money Grows
          on Trees

Day 3:   Brainstorm, Borrow, or Steal Ideas

Day 4:   Weigh the Obstacles and
          Opportunities of Each Idea

Day 5:   Forecast Your Profit on the
          Back of a Napkin

WEEK 2: SELECT YOUR BEST IDEA

Day 6:   Use the Side Hustle Selector
          to Compare Ideas

Day 7:   Become a Detective

Day 8:   Have Imaginary Coffee with
          Your Ideal Customer

Day 9:   Transform Your Idea Into
          an Offer

Day 10:   Create Your Origins Story

WEEK 3: PREPARE FOR LIFTOFF

Day 11:   Assemble the Nuts and Bolts

Day 12:   Decide How to Price Your Offer

Day 13:   Create a Side Hustle Shopping
          List

Day 14:   Set up a Way to Get Paid

Day 15:   Design Your First Workflow

Day 16:   Spend 10% More Time on the
          Most Important Tasks

**WEEK 4: LAUNCH YOUR IDEA
TO THE RIGHT PEOPLE**

Day 17:   Publish Your Offer!

Day 18:   Sell Like a Girl Scout

Day 19:   Ask Ten People for Help

Day 20:   Test, Test, and Test Again

Day 21:   Burn Down the Furniture Store

Day 22:   Frame Your First Dollar

WEEK 5: REGROUP AND REFINE

Day 23:   Track Your Progress and
          Decide on Next Steps

Day 24:   Grow What Works,
          Let Go of What Doesn't

Day 25:   Look for Money Lying Under
          a Rock

Day 26:   Get It Out of Your Head

Day 27:   Back to the Future

YOUR TURN: LET'S GET TO WORK!

By now you should have an idea of whether the hustling life is right
for you or not. Here's a quick test:

- ✓ Do you like the idea of having more than one source
  of income?
- ✓ Are you willing to devote at least thirty minutes
  a day to building your hustle, for at least the next
  twenty-seven days?

If you answered "Yes!" to those two questions, this plan is for you. Just one warning: Throughout the book, I'm going to be fairly direct in showing you what to do. I've hustled for more than twenty years, and I've worked with thousands of people starting their first hustle. I know what works and what doesn't. I want you to succeed, and I don't want to waste your time. Trust the process.

TRACK YOUR PROGRESS: FREE TOOLS

Last, while everything you need to succeed is in these pages, I've created some additional tools for those who want a little extra help in going through the model. The first is a free task-tracker to help you keep up with your progress. Sometimes it helps to have a visual reminder of how you're doing. Second is an online community where side hustlers like you can join up with other people who are all undertaking the challenge. You don't *have* to do this with a group, but many people find it beneficial.

Finally, I'll be posting additional resources online: just head to SideHustleSchool.com to register your copy of the book and get access to them.

Whether you love your job or can't stand it, everyone should have more than one source of income. And since you're the one making the decisions, it can also be fun—only unlike other things you do for fun, this form of entertainment actually *brings* you more money every month. Remember, a side hustle is the new job security. There's no downside, and the possibilities are unlimited.

Now let's turn this idea into your reality.

BUILD AN ARSENAL OF IDEAS

A side hustle has many benefits, but it all starts with an idea. This first week of hustling will teach you how to generate business ideas that actually work.

WEEK 1: BUILD AN ARSENAL OF IDEAS

Day 1: Predict the Future

Day 2: Learn How Money Grows on Trees

Day 3: Brainstorm, Borrow, or Steal Ideas

Day 4: Weigh the Obstacles and Opportunities of Each Idea

Day 5: Forecast Your Profit on the Back of a Napkin

DAY 1

Predict the Future

A side hustle has many benefits and no downside. It all starts with your answer to an important question: Twenty-seven days from now, what will be different about your life?

Before we get to work, let's get one thing straight. A side hustle isn't just about money in the bank, as helpful as that can be. A side hustle really can change your life. When you build something for yourself, even as you continue to work your day job, you become empowered. You gain confidence. You create security, both in the form of that extra cash and also in the fact that you're opening up future opportunities for yourself.

So right from the beginning of this journey, start thinking about your future. Assume that this side hustle thing will work out. What would that mean for you? What will be different about your life? Consider these three common goals of side hustlers. Which one speaks most to you?

GOAL #1: Make some extra cash for a specific purpose, whether to pay off a loan, buy a big-ticket item, take a vacation, or just build up your emergency fund.

GOAL #2: Create a sustainable and ongoing source of income that makes a real difference in your quality of life.

GOAL #3: Replace or exceed the income from your current job.

Note that these goals aren't *good, better, best*. Depending on your preferences and lifestyle, it may very well be the best decision to choose Goal #1 over Goal #2 or #3. Also, if you've started a side hustle before, the goal you had a few years ago may have changed, just as your overall situation in life changes over time. Side hustles are flexible and can fulfill different roles at different times.

As you select your goal, it may help to see how a few other hustlers made their decisions based on the goals they had set:

GOAL #1: Nick wanted to pay off a $2,500 loan. It wasn't a huge amount of debt, but it bothered him. Within a few short weeks after starting his first side hustle reselling classic video games, he was debt free.

GOAL #2: Bob and Barb, a middle-aged couple from Philadelphia, decided to work together on a side hustle, making custom baseball jerseys. It's a sustainable business that puts real money in their bank account each month—and it may even grow further—but they don't rely on it for their main source of income.

GOAL #3: Michael had been a teacher for ten years and wanted to make a transition to a life of self-employment. Fed up with the high cost of his cable service, he got the idea for a hustle to help people dramatically lower their bills. He got up at 4 a.m. every day to work on the project before his school day started, but it was worth the effort:

after a year he had grown his business to the point where he could quit his teaching job and strike out on his own.

Those are the major categories, but some side hustlers have more specific and personal goals: to establish a travel fund for themselves, to experiment with a project they may want to pursue further at some point, to support a charity they believe in, or something else. The possibilities are truly unlimited.

A side hustle is like a hobby, with one big difference: most hobbies cost money. A side hustle *makes* money. It's like playing entrepreneurially, getting paid to try something new and learn different skills.

Think ahead to that time twenty-seven days from now. If you follow this plan, at that point your hustle will be up and running. What will your life be like? Where will your hustle take you?

Learn How Money Grows on Trees

> Some hustle ideas are better than others. Learn
> the three qualities that make for a great idea, and
> understand how to find ones with the most potential.

San Diego graphic designer Julia Kelly wanted to make extra cash. After graduating from college she took a part-time summer gig as a caricature artist at a local amusement park. She'd always been good at sketching quickly, and drawing people sounded fun.

Despite her skills, Julia's summer job started with a terrifying experience: the park had a strict rule that artists couldn't sketch in pencil before committing to the finished product, so right from the start she had to use permanent markers. In other words, there was no undo button—no way to back up from a mistake or erase and start over. Drawing in front of a crowd of onlookers is intimidating, and even more so when you have to commit to each stroke from the beginning.

The trial by fire was intense, but it worked. After a few weeks, Julia no longer felt terrified. Instead, she felt confident. She'd mastered a new skill! She was rewarded with the smiles of happy children, as well as the gratitude of their parents who walked away with a tangible memory to place on the refrigerator or maybe even frame on the wall.

There was just one problem: the job paid only minimum wage, so her rewards mostly consisted of those smiles. Happy faces are nice, but you can't deposit them in your checking account.

Once the summer ended, Julia wanted to keep drawing portraits, but naturally she also wanted to make more money. That's when it hit her: maybe she could sell her services on her own somehow. She wrote to every school in the area, asking if they'd consider hiring her for their next event. After her fourth pitch, someone replied to say they had something coming up the same week. Could she bring her stash of markers and work for a few hours?

Indeed, she could. That event led to another, then another—and before long, she was charging $100 an hour for corporate events, a rate far higher than what she'd earned at the amusement park. That was a tremendous success on its own, but Julia wasn't finished. She had one more big idea that would catapult her earnings even higher.

With more experience, she had learned how to draw digital caricatures, a new form of media that hadn't been widely seen before. Instead of sketching with markers, Julia used a tablet computer. When she finished the drawing, she could print it out *and* email the image to the person, who often posted it to Facebook for all their friends to see.

This gave her work a "wow" factor that no other freelance artists in her area had, and the perceived value of her services skyrocketed. She began charging $250 an hour, focusing on corporate events that had larger budgets for the right kind of experiences. The higher rate was too much for some event planners, but plenty of others gladly accepted—so she was now making two and a half times as much while working the same hours. Julia's money tree was growing fast.

SOME IDEAS ARE BETTER THAN OTHERS

Once you understand that money really does grow on trees, the next step is to learn to plant the right seeds. The seeds for a money tree consist of moneymaking ideas. For your tree to bear fruit, you'll need to put in the work to turn those ideas into action. But your first step is to find the right ideas. They may not be obvious at first, but if you look closely, you'll find no shortage of *ideas that can be converted into money* available for the taking.

Every hustle starts with an idea—and for best results, you may need more than one. Before we go on, take note of an important fact about hustle ideas: not all of them are created equal. In fact, there's a tremendous range of potential profit among them. In Julia's case, one version of her idea paid $8 an hour, another paid $100, and another one paid a tremendous $250. It's obvious which approach was better.

Finding the best approach isn't always this simple because you're not always comparing ideas that are so similar. Still, almost every hustle idea that's worth pursuing shares three qualities. You want your idea to be *feasible, profitable*, and *persuasive*.

IS YOUR IDEA FEASIBLE?

Your goal is to start a project in a short period of time that earns money outside your day job. If any of these pieces of the equation are not immediately evident in the idea you're considering, you don't have a feasible idea.

Start A Project / That Earns Money / In A Short Period Of Time

START A PROJECT: you're actually going to do this, not just think about it. When you think about an idea, do you feel excited? Can you envision your next steps? If not, abandon the idea.

THAT EARNS MONEY: remember, a side hustle is not a hobby. A side hustle produces income. If you don't see a clear way to get paid, abandon the idea.

IN A SHORT PERIOD OF TIME: if your idea requires three years to get going, abandon the idea.

A feasible idea is one that you can turn into reality using the skills, time, and resources *you already have.* To put it simply, an idea that isn't feasible is not worth considering. Even if you don't know every step of the way, you must be able to see a pathway from idea to launch. In Julia's case, for example, she loved drawing caricatures and was good at it. She had both the skills and the desire to turn the idea into action. And because she knew that other companies regularly hired artists to draw portraits, she was confident her idea was something that people would pay for. Last, because her product required so little prep work, she also knew it was only a matter of days before she'd have her hustle off the ground.

IS YOUR IDEA PROFITABLE?

You're not looking for an idea that merely sounds interesting, you're looking for a *profitable* one. To make sure you understand the difference, consider two examples of entirely different ideas. Here's the first, from a personal chef with a love for high-quality desserts:

> *"I want to start an ice-cream-of-the-month club that delivers artisanal flavors to offices. The service is marketed to HR managers and small business CEOs as a way to increase morale and bring employees together for regular social experiences."*

In this example, there's a clear target market. Sure, the logistics of storing and delivering all that ice cream could get a little complicated, but it might be worth exploring if you knew how to source the ingredients and who your initial clients would be. This idea is at least *potentially* profitable, which is what you want.

Now consider another idea, from a college graduate beginning the slow climb at a consulting firm:

> *"I'd like to create an app that introduces a new form of payment for people who don't like credit cards or cash."*

Is that idea interesting? Sure, maybe. But how would you even begin to build and market it? It would be an enormous, expensive undertaking even if you had a background in both information technology and finance. And even if you could easily build it, how would you go about making it stand out from all the other payment apps on the market? At best, it's a grandiose vision that would require a great deal of dedication and struggle. That's not what a side hustle is about.

Here's another quick test: if you have a hard time explaining the primary benefit of your concept in more than a sentence or two, you may need to rethink the idea. If the primary benefit is unclear to potential customers, you won't convert many of them into *paying* customers

A side hustle is something that makes you money, not costs you money. If you don't see how you could make money from the idea, preferably in a short amount of time, it's probably not a good idea.

IS YOUR IDEA PERSUASIVE?

There's one more factor to consider as you brainstorm—and eventually select—your idea. It's not enough to have a good idea, even one that's potentially very profitable. Your idea has to arrive at the right time, and be so persuasive that it's hard for customers to say no to.

I recently went to an event where the parking cost $25. Normally it costs $5 to park in this lot, but for the special event the price had increased 500 percent overnight. Was I happy about paying $25 for something that usually costs $5? Nope. Did I pay it? Yep. Supply and demand ensured that the parking lot owner was providing a service that was very persuasive on that day.

Sometimes you'll have ideas that are just not ready yet. That's okay; you can hold on to them for later. Better to focus your current efforts on ideas that are persuasive *now*. To be successful, you want the right idea at the right time.

DISCOVER AND PURSUE HIGH-POTENTIAL IDEAS

Not every hustle idea is worth pursuing, and the ability to separate high-potential ideas from ones that are undesirable or merely interesting is a key skill of starting a profitable hustle quickly. With a bit of practice, you'll be able to do this right away.

Undesirable ideas have characteristics like these:

- A grand vision that is hard to simplify or translate into action

- Something you have no idea how to make (or requires skills that you don't have)

- A vague, nonspecific idea of the kind of people who will pay for it

- Something that is high maintenance or requires a lot of lead time to produce

High-potential ideas have characteristics like these:

- A simple path to turn the idea into reality that you can describe in one sentence

- Something that you know how to do or can easily figure out

- Solves a problem or makes someone's life easier in a specific way (*and* that they will be willing to pay for)

- Is low maintenance and easy to deliver without a ton of preparation or follow-up

- Will bring in income not just once but on a recurring basis

When considering different side hustle options, pass over ideas that are merely interesting. Choose high-potential ideas instead!

THE HIGH-POTENTIAL IDEA CHECKLIST

✓ Can you describe how to turn your idea into action in one sentence?
✓ Is there an obvious way to make money with this idea?
✓ Does this idea solve a problem for someone?
✓ Can you figure out how to make this idea happen quickly?
✓ Is it relatively low maintenance?
✓ Can you get paid more than once for this idea?

The more "yes" answers you have to these questions, the more potential your idea has. Can you say yes to *all* of them? Get to work right away!

Julia, the caricature artist, made a series of smart choices to go from temporary amusement park contractor to highly paid freelancer. Since drawing caricatures is an art form of its own, she first apprenticed at the amusement park to learn the ropes. Once she gained confidence, she moved from being a contract employee to freelancing, and her side hustle income rose from $8 an hour to $100 an hour. Finally, that hourly rate *skyrocketed* to $250 an hour when she learned a new form of media and begin offering something that no one else in the market had. The idea was feasible, profitable, and persuasive.

In May 2013, Julia quit her day job and began to live off her side hustle income, which was then bringing in more than $100,000 a year even though she typically only worked on-site at events one day a week.

Remember, you don't want ideas that are merely interesting. Whenever you have an idea, consider how feasible it is to get going and how profitable it might become. Consider as well if it's persuasive—is it the right idea *now*?

If you don't have any high-potential ideas yet, don't worry. By the end of the very next step, you will.

DAY 3

Brainstorm, Borrow, or Steal Ideas

> Side hustle ideas are all around you. Using
> what you've learned about high-potential
> ideas, it's time to brainstorm, borrow, or steal
> at least three possibilities for your hustle.

Dan Khadem works as a database programmer for a Colorado hospital. By sifting through complex information day in and day out, he's become really good at organizing that data in different ways. One of his most frequently used tools is Microsoft Access, a software program used widely in the healthcare world.

Access is a bit different from Microsoft Word or Excel, which are both designed to be user-friendly and don't require any specialized training. Anyone can pick up Access and get started, but to truly become proficient in it requires a lot of time and active study. Without some instruction, you'll likely feel overwhelmed.

For Dan, database programming came naturally. He had an engineering degree and had spent hundreds of hours exploring the ins and outs of the Access software. He had also adapted well to the world of side hustles. Since leaving high school, Dan had been financially responsible for himself and had accumulated more than $45,000 in the way of loans. He wanted to pay off those loans and begin saving for retirement, so he had begun pursuing a number of different hustles. He looked into the world of rental properties and eventually acquired two of them. He completed paid surveys and participated in research that paid a fee, taking advantage of his convenient location hospital worksite where a lot of these studies took place.

Dan knew that a lot of people used Microsoft Access every day, particularly in the healthcare world but also in the energy sector, the environmental industry, and elsewhere. So he signed up on a tutoring site where anyone with the right qualifications can offer tutoring services to students worldwide. Since his expertise was so specific, it didn't take long to get his first client. He decided to charge $55 an hour for online sessions, and $65 an hour if meeting in person.

Everything was going well—he tutored a few hours a week and made more than $500 a month on average, sometimes as much as $1,000 a month. But he also noticed that some of the students who came to him had other database needs that weren't being met merely through tutoring. These students needed more help or even a complete service. For example, some needed help building a custom database, and others required some more detailed form of consulting. Over time, the tutoring business became an entry point for this higher-level work, for which he charges somewhere in the range of $80–$125 an hour.

As with any side hustle, the extra money is great, but Dan also notes that the work has brought him additional benefits. "I like meeting people and forming new relationships," he told me. "People are very nice, especially when they look at you as the expert in something they need." He's also diversifying his skill set, gaining experience with a wider variety of programming functions than he uses in his day job—and getting paid to do it.

There's no doubt that Dan is a talented engineer and good with databases, but he also has an even more valuable skill: the ability to imagine and implement side hustle ideas. After all, not every hospital worker would think to earn $200–$300 a month by taking part in research studies. And not every computer engineer would see the moneymaking opportunity in tutoring students in database skills. Finally, not every online tutor would realize that his students might lead him to bigger opportunities for custom projects. Dan wisely recognized that a lot of professionals have to navigate large amounts of information, and they'd gladly pay to learn how to work faster and smarter.

To succeed in your side hustle, this is the kind of thinking you need to acquire.

IDEAS CAN BECOME ASSETS

Everywhere you look, hustle ideas are all around you. Many of these ideas can be exchanged for money. In creating your side hustle, the goal is to turn your idea into an asset, something that has real value and produces income for you over time. When you think of assets, your mind may go to things like stocks, bonds, and mutual funds. All of those are one form of assets, in the sense that with the right kind of effort, they can be turned into money.

Now imagine that a rich relative gives you a stock certificate that's worth a great deal of money, at least on paper. However, there's no way to exchange it into actual money if no one will buy it. It doesn't matter if that stock is supposedly worth a million dollars. If there's no way to exchange it into cash, you're not any better off than you were without it.

Side hustle ideas are like that stock certificate. They hold the potential for real value—but only if you cash them in. If they remain in your head or scribbled on the pages of your journal, the value remains trapped in the world of potential. Your goal as a hustler is to unlock that potential and start converting the idea into profit.

OK, SO LET'S GENERATE SOME IDEAS!

To get in the mindset of finding the profitable ideas that exist all around you, let's take an imaginary drive down the street and consider what kind of possibilities might appear. All along the way, pay close attention to your surroundings—you never know when a good idea might show up.

The first thing to notice is that we're not the only ones on the road. Who else is driving today, and where are they going? Are they driving to work or running errands? Here we can already spot several options.

First, all these people need to get somewhere. If you have a car and live in a city, you can sign up for a rideshare service and drive them where they need to go—even if you shuttle people around for just an hour before you have to get to your job. The good thing about signing on with these services is that you decide exactly when and how much you want to work. (Note: this might not actually be the *best* idea for you, but we'll get to that in a moment.)

Next, what about the people you see out your window who aren't driving? Maybe some of them are walking their dogs, lugging bags of dry cleaning, or carrying groceries. Many of these people might be willing to pay good money for help with these things, and there are several outsourcing services you can sign up for today that will put you to work. You can usually set your own rate, and as your reputation grows, you'll have more work and can charge a higher price. Or you can just start your own service, running around doing errands and collecting a second or third paycheck in your spare time.

Maybe you notice a line of people queuing up outside the local coffee shop. Or you see a cluster of cars piling up on the shoulder of the highway, in front of a sign for a full-service car wash. If you continue down this train of thought, asking yourself, *What are these people doing, and what do they need?*, you can likely spot several other opportunities:

- Deliver fresh coffee to people working in office buildings that aren't located on top of a high-end coffee shop.

- Set up a pop-up car wash service on the off-ramp of the highway (include a sign: FREE WI-FI WHILE YOU WAIT).

- Create a "life organization" service that helps busy people with planning their week and becoming more efficient when running errands.

Those ideas are fine to start with—but if you look closer, you'll begin to spot even better and more profitable ideas. After all, a side hustle shouldn't be just another part-time job. It should make your life easier, not harder.

Here's an example of a hustle that went beyond the "starter idea" approach of driving people around or washing their car. One day, a California web developer named Steven Peterson was commuting to work in the San Francisco Bay area, alongside tens of thousands of other people. California traffic during rush hour is no joke, and many of those commuters were constantly on the lookout for short-cuts, tips, or anything that would make their commute a little bit quicker and easier. At the time, there was no single, go-to resource where all these people could see traffic patterns and get real-time updates on buses, roadwork, or any other pertinent information. You'll read the whole story of what happened on Day 17, but the short version is that Steven built that resource and is now making more than $7,500 a month from it.

See how it works? In this case, Steven combined an existing skill (web development) with a clear need (real-time traffic information) that served a large and active market (San Francisco commuters). Steven now works full-time on the hustle, and it all started with an idea that popped into his head on his morning commute.

Now it's your turn. Try applying this mode of thinking wherever you go. Whenever you encounter groups of people, ask yourself *What do these people need or want?* And as you go through daily life, ask yourself, *What opportunities are lying in wait for someone to profit from?* In other words, look for ways to transform your ideas into valuable assets.

DIFFERENT KINDS OF HUSTLES

Generally speaking, there are three broad categories of side hustles. You can sell a product, whether one of your own or someone else's, you can provide a service, or you can be a middleman of some kind.

Selling a product is simple enough: you make, buy, or acquire something that you then sell to someone else. Products can be tangible (gourmet coffee) or intangible (traffic information). The point is that something is delivered, shipped, or otherwise transferred to someone else. Providing a service is also pretty simple: there's something you do for someone else, in exchange for payment. Whether running errands, coaching salespeople, or helping out with a tax return, when you do something for someone else, you're in the service business.

These two broad categories, selling a product or providing a service, have one big thing in common: customers or clients. Everything that you'll learn about creating offers, marketing the offers, and building a long-term customer base relates to them.

There's *also* one other broad category of hustles that have nothing to do with creating either a product or service—at least not directly.

Some very profitable hustles can be found in "decoding" or improving an existing process, improving it in a way that produces income *without creating a product and without directly serving any customers.* For example, on Day 25, you'll read about Trevor, a government analyst who operates a very successful hustle thanks to his mastery of a fulfillment program run by Amazon.com. He simply buys items at one price and resells them through Amazon at a higher one. Technically, he has customers, since there are real people buying his products—but he has no idea who they are, and in most cases they have no idea who he is, either.

This hustle exists because of an inefficient market. The items he buys (typically computers and electronic equipment) sell at different prices from different vendors. Trevor's goal is to buy low, sell high—or at least sell for a bit higher than what he paid.

If there were no differences in the price of the items Trevor purchases to resell, he wouldn't be able to make a profit.

The skills required to be successful in this kind of business are different from those required for more traditional product and service businesses. Trevor isn't necessarily an expert in anything he sells; he's an expert in the art of reselling, and in connecting the right sellers with the right buyers. There's not much that Trevor can do to improve his products, because he doesn't make them. He also can't really provide better service, because he doesn't do the shipping and doesn't even get a list of buyers' names.

But what he can do—and the way that he can make more money—is to keep improving his process of research and get better at figuring out which items to source and resell. As he gains more experience, he learns which items have the best profit margins, as well as which will sell the fastest. He then focuses on buying and reselling items that fit into at least one of those categories.

Hustles like these are all around you. Wherever money is exchanged, there's usually at least one way that a creative individual has found to make the process more efficient, and to profit from that improvement.*

---

* If you don't have an existing idea for something in this category, start with selling a product or providing a service. It's usually easier to brainstorm multiple ideas for either of those kinds of businesses.

STARTER IDEAS VERSUS NEXT-LEVEL IDEAS (NLIs)

As you learn to think more about hustle ideas, you'll notice other differences among them. Some ideas are "starter" ideas—they aren't bad, but they also have severe limitations. Then there are "next-level ideas" (NLIs) that have much better long-term potential.

On our imaginary drive, I mentioned ridesharing, where you essentially operate your own car as a taxi. A lot of people get started with side hustles by driving for Uber, Lyft, or some other rideshare service. It's not a bad start at all; you can work when you want, and the majority of the fares are yours to keep. Still, it also has a severe limitation: since you only make money when you're driving, you're still just earning an hourly wage that is capped by market demand, competition from other drivers, and of course, your own limited supply of free time.

In my last book, *Born for This*, I told the story of Harry Campbell, an Uber driver who created an online community called The Rideshare Guy. Instead of just ferrying people around all the time, he now also earns money coaching other drivers and serving as an expert commentator on the booming rideshare industry. This is what I mean by a next-level idea. See the difference? Since new drivers are signing up all the time, Harry's market demand is nearly inexhaustible.

> **Starter idea:** Drive for Uber
> **Next-level idea:** Coach other Uber drivers

As another example, back when I got started hustling more than two decades ago, I listed various items for sale on online auction sites. I started by listing random stuff from around my apartment that I no longer needed. It was fun and profitable, but it had a severe, built-in limitation: sooner or later I'd run out of stuff to sell!

I then learned to buy items from various auction sites and then sell them in another, earning a profit on the difference in price (much like Trevor did in the example above). That was a more sustainable idea, since my inventory was replenishable and I had the opportunity to buy lots of different kinds of items.

> **Starter idea:** Sell your own stuff
> **Next-level idea:** Buy other people's stuff, then resell for a higher price

If you're just getting started, starter ideas are totally fine. And if your hustling goal is just a onetime hit of cash, they may be all you need. Eventually, though, you'll probably want to shift your focus to NLIs. When you're choosing between two ideas and one of them is an NLI, that one is probably the better choice. And if you're not sure if your idea is an NLI, ask yourself if there's a built-in limit to the number of customers you can serve, or if it's a market that can be replenished over time. (More on this in Week 2.)

DON'T HAVE IDEAS? TAKE THESE

Side hustle ideas are all around you, but if you need help, I've compiled an initial list to get you started. Use them as starting points to inspire something you come up with yourself, tailor or adapt them to your skills or situation, or just steal them as they are.

- Sell your art, crafts, or any handcrafted item on etsy.com
- Develop a travel concierge service to help people when they miss their flights
- Offer online tutoring services in your field of expertise
- Host a networking event (charge a low ticket price and get sponsors to provide food)

- Create and sell a visitors' guide to your town or city, or build a web resource for tourists, supported by advertisers
- Create an online (or offline) course in some quirky subject you happen to know a lot about
- Publish a blog with a new lesson on a specific topic every day
- Start a podcast and sell sponsorship
- Visit yard sales or thrift shops and buy items to resell
- Offer a simple freelance service—anything from fact-checking to tech support or something else entirely
- Become a home, office, or life organizer
- Manage P.R. or social media accounts for small businesses
- Buy and sell used textbooks to college students
- Sell your musings on business, art, or culture as a freelance writer
- Start a membership website, where people pay a monthly or annual fee to access useful information about a specific topic
- Write and publish a book (if I can do it, you can too!)

Note: many of these ideas won't work for you. But some might! Go through the list and select any that sound promising. Most important, always be on the lookout for feasible, profitable, and persuasive ideas as you go about your daily life.

YOUR TURN: BRAINSTORM AT LEAST THREE QUALIFIED IDEAS

In the previous chapter, you learned how high-potential ideas need to be feasible, profitable, and persuasive. In this chapter, you learned how to generate lots of different ideas, and how to tell the difference between starter ideas and next-level ones. Now, using what you've learned, brainstorm and list at least three high-potential ideas.

These could be ideas you've been thinking about for a while, or ones that just came to you while reading these chapters.

You're not making any commitments yet; you're just getting things out of your head and onto paper so you can further explore them as we go along. If you need help, you can borrow, modify, or simply steal one or more of the ideas listed earlier (see pages 34 to 35).

Idea #1: _____

Idea #2: _____

Idea #3: _____

In the next step, we'll evaluate each of these ideas to see which has the fewest barriers to getting started quickly, and which has the most potential for making money. If you need to return to the idea-generation phase at any point, that's totally fine. But now that you're armed with three ideas, let's proceed to the next step of choosing which one you'll transform into an asset.

Weigh the Obstacles and Opportunities of Each Idea

Now that you have several ideas up your
sleeve, let's look at them more closely to
see which one has the most potential.

By day, Joe Maiellano works as the director of development at a
cancer research facility in Philadelphia. He's on the front lines of
the war against cancer, doing important work to help doctors and
scientists learn more about treating serious diseases.

In his spare time, Joe enjoys hanging out with his friend Jack.
Both of them have a "spirited" appreciation for cocktail culture,
and a few years ago they'd even gone so far as to collaborate on their
own homemade gin recipe (no bathtub needed). Then one day, presumably over drinks, they had what they thought was a great idea:
"Let's open a distillery and sell our gin to the world!"

Alas, this idea wasn't meant to be. When they looked into the
rules and regulations of operating a distillery, even a small one, they
discovered that all the red tape would pose a tremendous challenge.
Local, state, and federal agencies all controlled different aspects of
the alcohol trade, and it wasn't just a matter of paperwork: Joe and
Jack estimated that the startup costs for such an endeavor would be
in the one- to three-million-dollar range.

Disappointed but not deterred, Jack came up with the idea of selling people the tools to make their own gin in their own kitchens—a project that would require far less startup capital. And because Joe and Jack wouldn't be selling the actual alcohol, there were far fewer hoops to jump through, making the idea much more feasible to execute in a short period of time.

They started by assembling 250 "Homemade Gin Kits" in Joe's seven-hundred-square-foot condo, not having any real idea of who would buy them. But then the word got out. Thanks to their friends and family, as well as a few websites that featured the product, sales took off. They improved their operation, redesigned the website, and worked on the project during spare nights and weekends. The whole time, they kept working their day jobs.

Within four years, they had sold seventy-five thousand kits. Large kitchen stores ordered and stocked them. The *New York Times* wrote a favorable review. A friend mentioned having seen the kit at a major celebrity's home. By all accounts, their hustle had taken off.

To be fair, not everything is easy in the world of homemade gin. As the hustle grew into a real business, it wasn't only the press and lots of happy customers who noticed their success. A number of copycats sprang up, offering essentially the same product and some even duplicating their branding and sales copy with only minor changes. This was an annoyance, of course, but Jack and Joe recognized that it came with the territory of launching such a feasible, profitable, and persuasive project.

Overall, the two friends who started with a love of cocktails and followed a crazy idea couldn't be happier. Joe still has his day job, but he now also has the added security of a side hustle that makes real money and allows him to work on something he really enjoys—the best of both worlds. He never opened a distillery, but this turned out to be a much better outcome.

HOW TO IDENTIFY OBSTACLES AND OPPORTUNITIES

In the story of the Homemade Gin Kit, you can clearly see the *obstacles* that came with the initial idea to open a distillery, along with the *opportunity* that it also presented. If Joe and Jack had proceeded with their plan to produce and sell alcohol, they may well have turned a nice profit—but it would have been a much larger undertaking, and also a lot riskier. Since they didn't have three million dollars lying around (a major obstacle), they wisely abandoned the idea. However, their brainstorming produced another, better idea (a major opportunity, with fewer obstacles) that they decided to pursue.

Your ideas will also have obstacles and opportunities. You may not be able to see all of them at first—Joe and Jack didn't realize how hard it would be to open a distillery until they started looking into the process—but it's important to identify them as soon as you can. That's not to say that any opportunity with obstacles should be immediately abandoned, but rather that you should weigh them in the context of the potential for profit. That way, you'll not only select the best possible idea to act on, you'll also be more aware of what hurdles you have to overcome to make that idea a reality.

The makers of the Homemade Gin Kit used two simple strategies, brainstorming and research, to eliminate their first idea and pursue a far more feasible one. You can use these same strategies in your own hustle planning.

BRAINSTORMING. Just by applying a little logic, you should be able to immediately spot at least some obstacles and opportunities that are inherent in your service or product. Ask yourself, *What would be uniquely good, and what would be uniquely challenging about this project?* If your idea is to sell lunar golf carts to astronauts, you should understand right away that this idea comes with some major constraints: astronauts are a very small market, production costs are likely quite high, and it's hard to get to the moon to open your shop.

Similarly, if you think about who might benefit from your product and why, opportunities are generally easy to spot. Joe and Jack eventually chose to produce something that they knew a lot of cocktail enthusiasts might want. It helped that they essentially *were* their own target customers, and they wisely recognized that the kits would make a great gift. It wasn't necessarily *easy*, but it was a much better opportunity.

RESEARCH. Identifying the obstacles and opportunities in your idea may call for more formal research, but you don't necessarily need to head to the library and spend your weekends immersed in a stack of books. Joe and Jack's research process was pretty simple: they asked around and looked at a couple websites to learn more about local alcohol laws. Upon shifting their attention to the revised idea, their research simply consisted of exploring costs and coming up with some creative ideas to market their new gin kits.

Drawing on your own logical intuition and a small amount of research, you should be able to ask and answer questions like these:

- What will you need to get started, and how much will it cost?

- What potential obstacles stand in the way of launching your idea?

- How hard will it be for you to get your first sale?

- Has anyone ever done something like this before?

- If everything goes right, what's the best-case scenario?

- If everything goes wrong, what's the worst-case scenario?

As you narrow down your side hustle ideas, the more you can learn—and the more questions like these you can answer—the better your chances of moving forward with the highest potential one.

LET'S GET TO WORK

So far you've read about several different hustle ideas, including real-world projects and a few hypothetical scenarios. Let's look at a few other potential ideas, this time considering the obstacles and opportunities that each presents.

IDEA #1: HELP WEDDING PHOTOGRAPHERS PROCESS PHOTOS.

Constraints: Requires expertise and continuous manual effort (can't be automated), may be seasonal

Opportunities: Recurring market, the best wedding photographers are both booked solid *and* well paid, meaning that they are in a good position to pay for help

IDEA #2: COORDINATE A NETWORK OF NEIGHBORHOOD PET SITTERS; EARN COMMISSION ON EVERY BOOKING.

Constraints: Limited number of dogs, hard to compete with teenage labor

Opportunities: You're not actually pet sitting, you're matchmaking, which is far less time consuming (and also doesn't involve picking up after dogs or taking them for walks in the rain)

IDEA #3: BUILD A POPULAR PROFILE ON PINTEREST (OR ANOTHER NETWORK), EARNING ADVERTISING AND REFERRAL PROGRAM INCOME.

Constraints: Hard to get to an initial point of popularity, success is partially dependent on the size of the network

Opportunities: Can be done completely online from anywhere, easy to grow with outsourced help if it becomes popular

In the previous step, you selected at least three ideas—or maybe you borrowed some from me. Either way, drawing on what you've learned, make a quick list of each idea's obstacles and opportunities. For each idea, consider what would be *uniquely good* or *uniquely challenging* about it.

By understanding how easy or difficult your idea will be to implement, you'll have a much better understanding of which of your ideas to shelve, and which one you'll choose to move forward with. Next, we'll investigate how much profit potential each idea has. Don't skip this step: profit is good!

Forecast Your Profit on the Back of a Napkin

> To estimate the profit of your side hustle,
> you don't need a finance degree or a
> scientific calculator. You just need a napkin,
> a pen, and the power of observation.

There's a sharing economy service or app for everything these days. You can get paid to lend a set of tools to a neighbor you've never met. You can invest in a crowdfunding project led by strangers on a different continent. And now, several services let you rent out your car by the hour, day, or week to someone who needs it. If you have a car that you don't drive every day, it's one of the easiest ways to make some extra cash.

In Los Angeles, Tahsir Ahsan took this hustle idea several steps further. After creating an account with Turo, one of the sharing economy services that operates as a middleman between renters and car owners, he quickly learned how to optimize his price and listing details to bring him just about as much business as he could handle. Within a short period of time, his car was being rented an average of twenty-nine days every month—essentially all the time. Factoring in insurance and other costs, he was making more than

$1,300 each month simply for communicating with renters via email and managing the occasional airport pickup.

That's when he decided to raise the stakes. Some of us in this situation might think of renting out another vehicle, maybe even two if we were ambitious, but Tahsir decided to *lease an entire fleet of cars*—sixteen to be exact—and listed them all for rent. Each time he took care to price low for the first few rentals, to ensure that the car would be rented quickly and could generate immediate positive reviews. Then he gradually upped the price as the demand for his vehicles increased.

He was also smart about which kinds of cars he selected. Based on his research, he noticed that the best opportunities were either at the low end (renters who wanted the cheapest possible cars) or the high end (people who wanted to drive a nice car or SUV, perhaps for a weekend outing or to impress a date). Tahsir structured his car acquisition accordingly, choosing a few expensive cars and half a dozen cheaper ones. In fact, he got the cheaper ones during an incredible promotion when the manufacturer was overstocked on a particular model, the Chevrolet Cruze. "Imagine leasing a Chevy Cruze for $18 a month and renting it out for $35 a day," he wrote in a blog post. "You don't have to imagine it because that's pretty much what I'm doing."

To make it all work, he found a partner at an airline parking lot who would handle many of the pickups and returns for renters visiting from out of town. He spent a lot of time communicating with customers, but that back and forth was the majority of his hustle workload.

Leasing sixteen cars might seem like a pretty risky investment for a side project, but once Tahsir did the math based on his initial experience with one vehicle, he knew it would turn a profit—or at least he was fairly confident.

THE PROFIT EQUATION

The secret to turning a profit for any business or venture, whether it's a side hustle renting out cars or a multinational corporation, boils down to one basic principle: don't spend more money than you take in. With this principle in mind, the projected profit for just about any hustle can be calculated by the following simple equation:

EXPECTED INCOME - EXPECTED EXPENSES = PROJECTED PROFIT

Of course, to get the critical information of "How much money can I make with this idea?," you'll first need to make those estimates for income and expenses. To come up with your estimates for each factor, you'll usually need to identify several other variables. Using the car rental hustle example, let's say you're going to rent out a single car (a project that is approximately fifteen times easier than renting out sixteen cars). To reach an estimate for projected income, you'll need to make your best guess about two things:

AVERAGE DAILY RENTAL RATE: what someone pays to rent the car each day

NUMBER OF DAYS RENTED PER MONTH: how many days each month you'll rent out the car

**MONTHLY RENTAL INCOME =
DAILY RATE X NUMBER OF DAYS RENTED**

Then, you'll need to make your best guess about monthly expenses: lease, insurance, maintenance, commission to the service, and any other expenses. Consider a basic projection based on leasing a single car and putting it online for rental.

MONTHLY EXPENSES: LEASE + INSURANCE +
MAINTENANCE + COMMISSION

The final profit formula is simple:

MONTHLY RENTAL INCOME - MONTHLY EXPENSES = PROFIT

Now let's put the variables in a simple spreadsheet. Wait . . . did someone say spreadsheet? Yes, but don't worry. Scribbling it on the back of a napkin will also work; the spreadsheet format just makes the math easier.*

NAPKIN PROJECTION FOR RENTING ONE CAR

In this scenario, you could safely project monthly income of at least $300. No matter what you're selling, if you can get the Profit Equation to work, you have a successful hustle. Just like that!

ITEM	INCOME OR EXPENSE
Rental Income per Day (BEFORE EXPENSES)	$40
Expenses per Day	$13.30
Rental Income per Day (PROFIT)	$26.70
Days Rented per Month	20
MONTHLY INCOME (NET)	$534

Notice that you can change *any single variable* to affect the net result of your projection. If your net daily rental income is $26.70,

---

*   Head to SideHustleSchool.com to get a free downloadable spreadsheet where you can customize the numbers for your hustle. Bring your own napkin!

and you're able to go from twenty days rented per month to twenty-five, then you're suddenly making an additional $133.50 a month. Similarly, if you're able to increase your net daily rental income from $26.70 to $31.70 a day, you'll make an additional $100 a month even without increasing the total number of days rented.

NAPKIN PROJECTION WITH FIVE EXTRA DAYS RENTED

In this scenario, we adjusted the number of days rented per month, resulting in an extra $175 a month.

ITEM	INCOME OR EXPENSE
Rental Income per Day (BEFORE EXPENSES)	$40
Expenses per Day	$13.30
Rental Income per Day (PROFIT)	$26.70
Days Rented per Month	25
MONTHLY INCOME (PROFIT)	$667.50

NAPKIN PROJECTION WITH 15 PERCENT HIGHER RENTAL RATE

In this scenario, by adjusting the average rental rate, your projection increases by $100 a month.

There are lots of ways to play with estimates like this. The two examples above assume that only one variable changed. You could, however, make improvements in *both* the average rental rate as well as the number of days rented per month, and you'd see even more of an increase in profit. Nice!

However, your income could also be adversely impacted by higher expenses. Perhaps maintenance costs are higher than expected, thus lowering profits. Or maybe you're only able to rent for eighteen days per month instead of twenty, thus affecting the daily average as well as the monthly total. In this case, you might want to consider a slight rate increase, or seek another way to cut expenses.

ITEM	INCOME OR EXPENSE
Rental Income (BEFORE EXPENSES)	$45
Expenses per Day	$13.30
Rental Income per Day (PROFIT)	$31.70
Days Rented per Month	20
MONTHLY INCOME (PROFIT)	$634

The point is that by forecasting profit and expense with a simple estimate like this, you'll be able to make decisions for your hustle with far more confidence than you would simply by guessing.

WHAT ABOUT WHAT YOU DON'T KNOW?

Many times, your back-of-napkin analysis won't be as straightforward as the above example. Even with his fleet of sixteen rental cars, Tahsir was able to project the revenue with great accuracy. That's because there was very little hidden information in that scenario. He knew how much the leases and insurance would cost. He also had a pretty good estimate of monthly income, based on an average rental rate per day as well as the average number of days per month that each car would likely be rented.

But in cases where you *don't* have all the info, you'll need to do a little extra legwork to figure out what *will* make your hustle profitable.

Let's say you want to teach a class. The topic of your class will be something you know a lot about—bird-watching or rocket science, perhaps. You're not sure exactly how much you should charge for the class (on Day 12, you'll learn about pricing your offer based on your minimum acceptable income), but you're considering something in the range of $49 to $79. Your friend will lend you his basement as a location for the class, so you have virtually no expenses.

To figure out the profit potential for this hustle, the only factors you need to consider are the cost of the class and the number of signups. The formula looks like this:

$$(\text{PRICE}) \text{ X } (\# \text{ OF SIGNUPS}) = \text{PROJECTED PROFIT}$$

Since the decision of what to charge is entirely up to you, the main "unknown" in this scenario is the number of people you think you can get to sign up. But how do you get to that estimate? Because you've already identified your built-in constraints and opportunities, you'll be able to take a general guess. For now, decide on the minimum number of students you'd need to have at the lowest acceptable rate for the class to be worth it to you. If you can get more students (or charge more), that's great, but let the minimum number of students be your baseline.

MAKE A RANGE OF PROJECTIONS

How do you know if your projections are accurate? Much of the time, you won't know until you launch and see how people respond. So unless you're confident that you can accurately predict both (a) your net income (price minus expenses) and (b) how many customers you'll have, don't just do one projection. In addition to the original one, make an "optimistic" projection based on strong results, as well as a "conservative" one based on weak results. It's not three times as much work to do this; you can usually arrive at the optimistic and conservative projections by changing a single variable. In the rental car example, we could simply adjust the number of days per month a typical vehicle would be rented.

ORIGINAL ESTIMATE: 25 days per month
CONSERVATIVE ESTIMATE: 21 days per month
OPTIMISTIC ESTIMATE: 28 days per month

Similarly, in the bird-watching class, your projection will change based on either the number of students, the price charged for the class, or both. Let's use the formula to consider a range of outcomes:

RANGE OF PRICES WITH FIVE STUDENTS ($49, $59, $79)

In this scenario, we adjusted the cost of the class. The number of students stays the same, but your profit increases because each student pays more.

Cost of Class	$49	$59	$79
# of Signups	5	5	5
PROJECTED PROFIT	$245	$295	$395

FIXED PRICE WITH RANGE OF STUDENTS (5, 10, 15)

In this scenario, we adjusted the number of signups for the class. Notice that even if you keep the cost at $49, you'll end up making more money simply as a result of having more signups.

Cost of Class	$49	$49	$49
# of Signups	5	10	15
PROJECTED PROFIT	$245	$490	$735

As with Tahsir's fleet of rental cars, you can also adjust more than one variable at a time. If you charged $59 instead of $49 *and* saw an increase from five to ten students, for example, your projected profit for the class would rise from $245 to $590.

DON'T WAIT TO FIGURE OUT
HOW A SIDE HUSTLE WILL MAKE MONEY

There's an old joke about a bar in Silicon Valley, the original hub of the startup scene. A bar opens and is wildly popular—sort of. A million people walk into it, but don't buy anything. The bar then declares massive success, and the founders "exit" by selling their company to a group of investors.

It's a good joke that reflects a very bad business experience. It doesn't matter how many people walk into your bar; what matters is how many people buy something. An overfunded startup may be able to play hard and fast with the central law of economics (don't spend more than you make), but for a scrappy side hustler, this is not a winning strategy.

Your side hustle absolutely must have a clear plan to make money. Don't set aside this requirement and decide that you'll "figure it out later." That's fine for a hobby, but not for a hustle.

If you're still weighing several ideas at this point, you'll want to do some profit calculations for each one. Don't worry about being on-the-nose accurate; the goal is to *compare the profit potential of your various ideas* to see which one might be more worthwhile to pursue.

Any idea that doesn't have a likely path to profit should be abandoned. Money isn't everything, but when it comes to a side hustle, money matters a lot.

WEEK 1 RECAP!

After reading this week's steps, you should have several potential ideas in mind for your hustle. You should have weighed the constraints and opportunities and calculated the profit potential for each one. If you *don't* have any ideas yet, read through the first five days again. In Week 2, we're going to decide which of these ideas to turn into action, so move on to the next section only when you have several ideas that you can compare and rank against one another.

—   KEY POINTS   —

- Money grows on trees, but you have to plant the right seeds. Start to notice potential opportunities wherever you go.

- Not all hustle ideas are created equal. For best results, your ideas should be feasible, profitable, and persuasive.

- Starter ideas are fine for a while, but at some point you'll want to transition to NLIs (next-level ideas).

- Use the back-of-napkin financial analysis (or a simple spreadsheet) to estimate the profit of your idea (or ideas) before proceeding further.

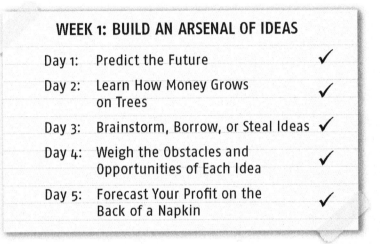

WEEK 1: BUILD AN ARSENAL OF IDEAS

Day 1:   Predict the Future   ✓

Day 2:   Learn How Money Grows
         on Trees   ✓

Day 3:   Brainstorm, Borrow, or Steal Ideas ✓

Day 4:   Weigh the Obstacles and
         Opportunities of Each Idea   ✓

Day 5:   Forecast Your Profit on the
         Back of a Napkin   ✓

SELECT YOUR BEST IDEA

Once you have multiple ideas, you need to be able to identify the best ones. Learn how to instantly rank and compare ideas so that you'll have confidence to proceed with the highest possible odds of success.

WEEK 2: SELECT YOUR BEST IDEA

Day 6: Use the Side Hustle Selector to Compare Ideas

Day 7: Become a Detective

Day 8: Have Imaginary Coffee with Your Ideal Customer

Day 9: Transform Your Idea Into an Offer

Day 10: Create Your Origins Story

Use the Side Hustle Selector to Compare Ideas

Once you start thinking about side hustles, the ideas don't stop. This tool will show you how to apply "Tinder for Hustling" logic to pick the best one at any given time.

Nearly one hundred years ago, the first Waldorf school opened in Stuttgart, Germany. It was novel for its time, and in some ways still is: the method emphasizes the role of imagination in learning and encourages teachers to foster creative as well as analytical thinking. The pace of learning is set according to developmental stages, in addition to the usual classroom grades. Since then the Waldorf model has spread all over the world, with thousands of schools operating in more than sixty countries.

Meredith Floyd-Preston is a proud Waldorf teacher in Oregon, and for years has immersed herself in studying and developing the most effective curriculum for her students. She's also been a reliable resource for other teachers, especially new ones who aren't used to the novel approach that the Waldorf method requires. All this hard work led her to an observation: designing custom lessons takes a lot of time! A key element of the Waldorf approach is that the teacher prepares curriculum herself, rather than teaching from a textbook—but for busy teachers, this can be incredibly time-consuming and tedious.

In looking for ways to lighten this workload, both for herself and her fellow teachers, Meredith noticed that a few curriculum resources were available for purchase, but only by schools, not individual teachers. Furthermore, the Waldorf method was becoming increasingly popular within the homeschooling movement, but homeschooling parents didn't usually have the same training that credentialed instructors did, and they had even less access to resources.

Meredith had been searching for a side hustle. As an active knitter and web designer in her spare time, she was good at working on multiple projects at once. Helping fellow teachers and homeschooling parents save time and teach better lessons was not only a worthy goal, she thought; it might also be a profitable one.

Deciding on the right approach required some analysis. She thought about offering consulting or coaching sessions, but that didn't seem feasible. Teachers were busy people (which is why they needed help) but Meredith was busy, too, and one-on-one coaching sessions were a huge time commitment. She also thought about creating a live workshop, which would allow her to reach more teachers at once—but the profit potential would still be low, since she could only be in one place at one time. A third option, creating curriculum guides for online purchase, was the most attractive. The guides would be low-priced, so she wouldn't earn much on any individual sale, but they were far more scalable, meaning that what she lacked in profit margin she could make up in volume. Also, once they were complete and uploaded, whatever she earned would be nearly all profit.

She decided to go for it. After writing her guides and compiling them in a simple PDF format, she put them online and quietly let people know they were available. When the initial response proved favorable, she began thinking about creating a whole series of planning documents for sale, another project that would require effort on the front end but then become pure upside with no further work required.

Meredith had found an approach that was feasible, profitable, and persuasive. Because new teachers were coming on board with the Waldorf approach each year, there was a virtually inexhaustible supply of customers. For Meredith, this side project was the perfect match.

"TINDER FOR SIDE HUSTLES"

The world of online dating is estimated to be a two-billion-dollar-a-year industry. With so much at stake, it's no surprise that the most successful dating websites invest tremendous amounts of money in fine-tuning their "matching" algorithms. They know that the average person who is seeking a partner, whether for life or for something more short term, doesn't want to be served up a random selection of uninterested or uninteresting people—they want to see a limited selection of people *who might actually be good for them*. These businesses thrive when they provide ideal matches, not just an infinite and unfiltered pool of strangers.

It's not about *more options*, in other words, it's about *better matches*.

How can you apply "Tinder for Hustling" logic to your planning? You look at a lot of ideas, rejecting most of them, flirting with a few, and then—hopefully—settling in for a trial phase with the most attractive and well-rounded option. In the first section, you learned how to generate ideas. Now you'll learn a simple algorithm you can use to compare these ideas and find your ideal match. Fortunately, it's usually a lot easier than finding your soul mate.

THE SIDE HUSTLE SELECTOR:
HOW TO RANK AND COMPARE YOUR IDEAS

If you already know the hustle you're going to commit to during the twenty-seven-day plan, great! But since a key part of hustling is learning to brainstorm and generate multiple ideas, it's still worth learning how to weigh ideas against one another in search of the best possible one at any given time.

In that first week, you learned about feasibility, profitability, and persuasion, three critical qualities for successful hustles. A quick refresher:

FEASIBILITY: The ability to begin turning the idea into action in a short period of time

PROFITABILITY: The potential to make money from this idea, also in a short period of time

PERSUASION: Not only is this a good idea, it's a good idea *now*

To narrow our list even further, let's add two more qualities to the mix:

EFFICIENCY: How quickly can this be executed?

MOTIVATION: How excited are you about this idea?

Time is important because you don't have a lot of it—so you'll want to choose an idea that is as efficient as possible. Second, motivation also matters. Your side hustle should be at least a *little* fun, if not a lot. You don't want to burn out on it. You want it be something you look forward to, not something you dread or treat like a chore.

To make an immediate comparison between multiple ideas, you'll want to apply a High, Medium, or Low ranking to each of these five qualities. It's pretty straightforward: based on the information available to you, ask yourself how the idea scores in each quality. Then, fill in the blanks in a table like this:

YOUR IDEA HERE		
	High	Medium	Low
Feasibility			
Persuasion			
Profit Potential			
Efficiency			
Motivation			

Like the back-of-the-napkin profit tool, you can do this analysis very quickly. You may have to guess at some of the rankings, since not all information is known in advance, but that's okay. The point is to compare multiple ideas to see if a clear winner emerges. If one idea clearly ranks higher on most qualities, it's a pretty good indication that that's the one to try.

Let's use Meredith's story as a test case to see exactly how the Side Hustle Selector works. She had already identified a clear need: to help Waldorf teachers save time and improve their teaching. As a Waldorf teacher herself, with a long-standing love of curriculum, she was also highly qualified to meet that need. But *how* would she do it? Several opportunities were possible: in-person coaching sessions, live workshops, and curriculum resource guides (the idea she eventually settled on).

For the sake of simplicity, imagine she was torn between the in-person coaching sessions and the curriculum resource guides. By using the Side Hustle Selector, she'd be able to quickly compare and contrast the two ideas. Here's the first:

IDEA #1: IN-PERSON COACHING FOR TEACHERS			
	High	Medium	Low
Feasibility		X	
Profit Potential			X
Persuasion	X		
Efficiency			X
Motivation		X	

On the other hand, Meredith knew she was a qualified authority in the world of Waldorf curriculum. She also knew teachers needed help, making her idea highly persuasive. In thinking about all that was involved in the first hustle idea, a series of in-person coaching sessions, Meredith realized it wasn't really feasible. The time commitment would be high (since she'd have to be physically present for the sessions), and she already had a packed schedule. Furthermore, the profit potential was low, since she could only do a limited number of sessions, and she didn't want to charge teachers a high price. And the fact that she could only conduct one session at a time made the whole thing rather inefficient. As for motivation, it might not have been the most exciting idea she ever had, but she was certainly enthusiastic and committed to making it happen.

Now let's look at the same analysis of her idea for the curriculum guide.

IDEA #2: CURRICULUM GUIDES FOR SALE			
	High	Medium	Low
Feasibility	X		
Persuasion	X		
Profit Potential		X	
Efficiency	X		
Motivation		X	

For the sake of a quick comparison, let's assume that several factors were the same in the second idea: both ideas were equally persuasive, and Meredith was equally motivated for each one. But in the second idea, three key factors were different: because the guides would be sold online to anyone who needed them, the profit potential was higher—and once the guides were written, the required time to maintain them was very low. This made for an idea that was not only more efficient, but more feasible given all the other demands on Meredith's time. With three marks in the "high" category, the curriculum guides were the clear winner.

You can customize this basic Side Hustle Selector tool in different ways. One option is to weight certain variables based on what's most important to you at the time. For example, if profit is the most important factor for you at the moment, you could assign it double the value. Or, for a more finely tuned analysis, you could also rank the qualities on a scale of 1 to 10 instead of just choosing Low, Medium, or High. The important thing is to be consistent so you don't end up comparing apples to oranges. Remember, your goal is to rank and compare different ideas, then select the best candidate.

STILL INDECISIVE? READ THIS

If you're like me, you may sometimes have trouble choosing among all your different side hustle ideas. I want to do it all! To avoid decision-making paralysis, remember these three guidelines.

1. You're not making a lifelong decision, you're looking for the right idea at the right time. Save all your other ideas for later—you may end up coming back to them at some point.

2. Hang on to those extra ideas, but never save your *best* idea for later. Use the selector tool to figure out which idea is strongest and has the most potential, and then lead with that.

3. If you still can't decide after all the analysis, just pick what feels right at the moment. When it comes to side hustles, action is almost always better than inaction. Even if you end up changing course later, you're still gaining valuable experience and building valuable skills.

The road to side hustle paralysis is paved with good intentions. Don't get stuck on that road—pick an idea and keep trucking along.

FINAL CHECKLIST FOR THE IDEA

If your head is still buzzing with ideas, that's good, but it's even better to turn your best idea into a moneymaking reality. From everything you've read or thought of thus far, select your best idea. Abandon or shelve other ideas for now. We're moving forward with the best possible option! Are you almost ready to get to work on a real-life side hustle? Let's do a quick review to find out.

- ✓ Do you have an idea you can explain in very simple language?
- ✓ Is your idea feasible, profitable, and persuasive?
- ✓ Is it clear how the idea will make money?
- ✓ When you think about the idea, does it make you feel excited?

Ideally you want to be able to say "Yes!" to each of these questions, or at least most of them. If you aren't there yet, keep considering and evaluating different options. Your odds of success will be much higher if you're prepared to roll up your sleeves and get to work on your idea immediately after completing this step. It's time to start turning this idea into action.

Become a Detective

> As you move forward with an idea, take a
> look at what other people are doing. Then,
> do it better—or at least differently.

When Andrea Hajal moved to Texas from her native Spain, she gained true love but left behind her beloved pets. Her fiancé was from the United States, and after traveling together for a couple years, they decided to marry and settle down in Austin. Andrea enjoyed her work as a nutritionist, but her real love was animals, especially dogs. One day while she and her fiancé were staying in a rental apartment on a trip to Canada, she had an idea: "What if there was something like Airbnb, but for dogs? You know, so their owners could travel and leave the dogs somewhere better than a kennel?" A year later, she stumbled on Rover.com—a service that did exactly what she'd described, essentially providing a platform where animal-loving hosts could rent their spare doggie bed out to canine guests.

Andrea eagerly created a profile, advertising her home as a welcoming place for dogs of all breeds. She loved caring for dogs, but she also had enough business savvy to recognize that with dozens of other dog-loving hosts competing for bookings on the site, her caretaking skills alone wouldn't be enough to turn this venture into a successful side hustle. So she started doing a little detective work: carefully studying the profiles and reviews of other dog landlords, paying close attention to what the successful ones did differently from the rest.

One thing she quickly noticed was that the most popular dog sitters had not just one, but several photos on their profile pages. So she went above and beyond, posting more than fifty photos of herself playing with dozens of different dogs. Before long, she had her first booking, then another, and many more. After her customers (the owners, not the dogs) posted rave reviews, she began to have bookings almost every day. The side hustle became a way for her to enjoy the company of dogs again, something she'd missed since leaving Spain. It also produced an average of $80 a day, and sometimes up to $200 a day during holiday weeks—not bad for a part-time gig.

RECONNAISSANCE MISSION

Before choosing a retail location for a new café or store, most aspiring business owners undertake a detailed survey of the surrounding area. What's the neighborhood like? Where do people gather, and where do they spend money?

The owner of the new café probably doesn't want to open in a small neighborhood that already has three coffee shops on the same street. Too crowded! However, she may not want to be the only café in the area, either. It's not always good to be the pioneer; sometimes it's better to go where the people are.

Like the prospective café owner, you should probably do some reconnaissance on the competitive landscape before committing to your idea. Take time to understand your new neighborhood, and think about where you can make a home for yourself in it.

Your reconnaissance mission doesn't need to be complicated. You just want to learn two things:

1. Who else is offering the same thing or something similar

2. How your idea will be better or different

Does what you plan to offer already exist in some fashion? If so, learn as much as possible about those existing businesses. What do they do right *and* wrong?

Once you've done that, you want to identify something that you can do better or differently than the competition. You don't have to be better at *everything*—in fact, you probably won't be. When you closely observe the competition, though, you may be able to pick up on some things that they either haven't noticed or just haven't had time to address. For example, when Andrea set up her "Airbnb for dogs" hustle, she noticed that the most popular dog sitters on Rover.com had several nice photos on their profiles. You might think she was being excessive in posting more than fifty photos of herself frolicking with dozens of furry friends, but for someone who's deciding between dog hosts, the mere fact that Andrea was motivated and diligent enough to post so many photos could be a huge point in her favor.

Similarly, Andrea noticed that the dog-hosting platform encouraged sitters to send photos of dogs to their owners while the owners were away. The platform also tracked and posted how frequently this occurred, as well as the average time it took hosts to respond when owners inquired about their pets. This observation produced two more goals: Andrea would aim for a 100 percent photo-sending rate, and a very speedy one-hour response time. By paying attention to these goals, over time she shot up to the very top of the listings, frequently appearing in the top five of more than forty potential sitters in the area.

FOLLOW THE MONEY

When there are already other businesses in the same field you're entering, often you can do some simple things to learn more about how they operate. You can visit their websites, read their customer reviews, check out their social media postings, or maybe even try out the product or service yourself. In some cases, however, you may have to do a little more detective work to find out how much those established businesses cost to get going, and how much money they bring in. Back when I was first selling on online auctions, I paid attention to the kinds of items that sold over and over. Then I tracked down the wholesalers or distributors of those items, and then I inquired about their prices. From there it was pretty easy to see not only what was selling and for how much, but also what the original price for the seller was. If it seemed like a profitable opportunity, I would then place an order from the wholesaler and create my own listings.

It's not always that simple, of course. When you "follow the money," your goal is not only to determine roughly how feasible and profitable the idea is, but also what your competitors are doing that's making them money. Then, you want to figure out *how you can adopt and improve on their strategy.*

When Andrea paid close attention to the most popular listings, in addition to learning that average response time was critical, she also learned that successful dog sitters didn't just board dogs in their homes—they were also available for other services, like drop-in visits and walking dogs while their owners were at work. She added those services to her listing and saw a 20 percent increase in weekly income.

VALIDATE AN IDEA WITH $10 AND A FACEBOOK ACCOUNT

Do you have $10? Have you ever used Facebook? I'm guessing the odds are 99 percent or higher that the answer to both questions is yes. If you have a big idea and want to get some real-world feedback (not just from your friends) before going further, you can set up an advertisement and see how people respond. No need to rent a billboard—with Facebook you can get it going in less than an hour and as little as $10.

In Appendix 2, you can read a ten-step plan on how it works. The details are a little technical, so I've also included a link to a website with screenshots.

WHAT IF YOUR HUSTLE IS THE FIRST OF ITS KIND?

Even if your hustle is entirely new and there's nothing to compare it to, you can still find ways to make it stand out. When you're making or offering something that has never been done before, you'll want to make sure it's very easy to explain and understand. Convincing people that they want to buy something they've never heard of and didn't know they needed is challenging, so you'll have a *great* advantage if your concept is crystal clear and very easy to understand.

Consider a few examples, all taken from the research for this book:

- Homemade Gin Kit (see Day 4)

- Decorative Plaques Hand-Carved in the Shape of Pennsylvania (see Day 21)

- Custom Candy Hearts (see Day 11)

As different as they are, these concepts have two important qualities in common. First, they're *simple*. From a single sentence, or even just a few words, you know exactly what they are. Second, these items all have a clear benefit: they are fun. This is key because people are naturally resistant to spending money when they don't understand how the purchase will help them. True, you don't *need* any of them—life will probably continue its usual course if you don't start making gin in your bathtub, for example. Yet these offers were still persuasive because there was an immediate, understandable benefit to potential buyers.

It wasn't that hard for Andrea to get her "Airbnb for dogs" business up and running—she had her first doggy day-care booking within a week. But then she went above and beyond, doing everything she could to make the best possible impression on prospective puppy parents. She continued to post lots of photos and respond to inquiries quickly, mostly because that helped to reassure dog owners, but also with an eye on the platform's algorithm that rewarded more active engagement.

That kind of attention to detail, drawn from her observations of why some dog landlords did much better than others, set her apart.

Before long, she'd built a strong following throughout the area, with rave reviews from everyone who hired her. When she went to visit family in Spain for a month, she turned off the account, then turned it back on upon her return—and had three new bookings the first day. Her customers had missed her, and she quickly moved back to the top of the local listings. The Airbnb for dogs was open for business once again.

Have Imaginary Coffee
with Your Ideal Customer

There's one person out there who fits the profile of
your target customer. What can you learn from them?

Day after day, Shannon Mattern got out of bed and dragged herself to a dull, windowless office dominated by variations of beige.
Beige walls, a beige desk, and what felt like a beige life. She often
felt drained, depressed, and imprisoned by her job doing IT work.
Shannon needed a change, and she knew that change wasn't going
to fall out of the sky. If she wanted things to be different, she'd have
to stop complaining and start taking action.

One day while completing the dreaded monthly report fil-
ings she had to compile, she noticed that a Wordpress site she had
built for her employer had pulled in $7,000 worth of business that
month. She knew that she could put together a similar site in under
a week—but who would hire her?

At her day job, Shannon was the go-to tech guru, and she'd been
building websites for the better part of eight years. She'd noticed
that a lot of people had interesting business ideas, but they lacked
the skills to put together an appealing website to attract clients.
With that observation, a side hustle idea was born.

One day at the gym, she got to talking with a woman who asked what she did for a living. Shannon mentioned that she did IT work for a nonprofit and freelance web design on the side—despite not having any actual clients.

The other woman mentioned that her business was looking for someone to help them upgrade their website and suggested that they meet up for coffee. That single conversation landed Shannon her first gig working on another company's website, and she began to think more about using her skills to make money on the side. The only problem was that design work took a lot of time, and she already had a day job.

That's when she decided instead of building websites for people, she'd show them how to do it themselves, using the popular Wordpress platform. It was surprisingly easy to get started. The very day she posted a link to a free course in a Facebook group for entrepreneurs, someone signed up for her mailing list. That person then purchased a product she recommended, and Shannon earned a commission on the sale. Right away she knew she was on to something that people needed.

She called her side hustle "Wordpress BFF" and positioned it as an alternative to general consulting or all-purpose tech help. When I asked Shannon how she imagined her most likely customer, she ran through a list of features: a woman in her mid-twenties or early thirties who wants to have more control over her schedule and income. She may want to travel, or stay home with her kids, or simply run a business from home—or she may have no idea what she wants to do but *does* know that she's not fulfilled with what she's doing now.

As Shannon finished sketching out this detailed description of her customer, she paused. Then a lightbulb went off. "Oh wait, that's me!" She was her own ideal customer and therefore understood that person's needs better than anyone. Once she came to this realization, she began to focus her time on courses and products geared toward people just like her. By the end of the first year of her hustle, she earned more than $20,000. By midpoint of year two, she had already crossed $30,000, all while reducing the actual design work she did in order to focus on more passive income. She was still working her day job but found her side hustle so fulfilling that her life suddenly didn't look as beige anymore.

START WITH ONE

Every side hustle has a target customer, a specific type of person that its product or service is designed for. Sometimes these target customers are called "avatars," but you can also just think of them as *your people*. And the better you can understand those people—who they are, what they need, and where their pain points are—the better equipped you'll be to serve them.

Consider an example of someone else who found success only when he figured out who "his people" were. When John Lee Dumas of San Diego started a podcast called Entrepreneur on Fire, he had high hopes. He wanted to gain a large audience and reach a lot of people. There's nothing wrong with that vision, but in starting out he made a critical, yet common mistake. In defining his audience so broadly, he failed to crystallize a clear vision of whom the podcast (and eventually the community) was actually for.

Three months in, he'd seen some success, and he liked the medium of podcasting. He knew he could stick with this hustle for the long term. But John Lee also felt like he needed to sharpen his focus, so he started thinking about who his listeners were. But then he went even further. It wasn't just about identifying his listeners, he thought. Somewhere out there was an ideal *listener*, a single person for whom his Entrepreneur on Fire podcast was perfectly suited.

He took out a piece of paper and began writing about that imaginary person. He called him "Jimmy," and he added a ton of details about him. Jimmy was thirty-four years old and a married father of two kids. His wife was a stay-at-home mom, and every day Jimmy drove exactly twenty-seven minutes to his office, where he worked from a cubicle.

Like Shannon, the real-world IT employee, imaginary Jimmy didn't love his job. He dutifully performed the work his boss assigned, but he also spent a lot of time watching the clock. When it struck 5 p.m., he was out the door. When he got home he exercised, spent time with the kids, had dinner with the whole family, and then relaxed for an hour or two in front of the TV. When he wasn't entranced in the latest sitcom, Jimmy felt troubled. *Why am I doing this?* he wondered. *Isn't there something better?*

Also like Shannon, he wanted to change, maybe even quit his job and start his own business, but he didn't know how. He felt alone with his many questions, since all his friends were fellow corporate employees who had never traveled down the entrepreneurial path that Jimmy was increasingly curious about.

By the time he was finished jotting down all these notes about "Jimmy" (and more—those are just the highlights), John Lee had written more than thirteen hundred words. The exercise helped him feel like he had a much better handle on his audience: who they were, what they cared about, and what they wanted. He made subtle adjustments to his show, focusing on key actions and points of inspiration that would help "Jimmy" gain confidence and begin taking the first steps toward entrepreneurship.

He calls this method "Start with one." It's built on the key principle that there is one person—whether you call it your avatar or your ideal customer—who desperately needs what you have to offer. Start thinking about that person, and focus entirely on serving them.

People often think, "I don't want to leave anyone out," John Lee told me. "But that's wrong! This is scarcity thinking. When you focus all your efforts on that one person who is perfect for you, you'll actually end up serving many more."

On the first day of his podcast relaunch, John Lee had three downloads. One was from him, and one was from his girlfriend. In his mind he thought of that third download as being from "Jimmy," his ideal customer. Six hundred episodes later, each one now regularly gets downloaded thirty thousand times or more. He traces this success to being extremely specific about the people he serves, starting with that imaginary guy.*

Interestingly, since starting up he's also received many grateful emails from people who sound exactly like Jimmy. He started with one, and over time grew to serve many.

WRITE A LETTER TO YOUR IDEAL CUSTOMER

When John Lee Dumas wrote thirteen hundred words about Jimmy, his ideal podcast listener, it helped him gain a clear understanding of the people he wanted to serve. The description even included the names and ages of Jimmy's imaginary children, how he liked to exercise, and what he watched on TV when he came home from work!

You may not be able to get *that* detailed in describing your avatar, but don't skip the most important part: understanding the pain that he or she is going through. In "Jimmy's" case, that pain was his day job. Every day he spent hours trapped in the cubicle, not finding any meaning in the work but having to do it anyway to support his family.

If you have an idea of who your customer is, but are having trouble figuring out their pain points, it may help to have an extended (albeit one-way) conversation with them. One way to do this is to write a letter to your ideal customer and show them you understand their needs. Propose a solution and build a relationship with this imaginary person. The more you know

---

* He's also worked very hard—it's no small accomplishment to produce more than six hundred back-to-back episodes.

who they are—and of course, how you can help them—the more successful your side hustle can be. To read a sample customer letter, along with an analysis of which parts are the most important, head over to Appendix 3.

GO BEYOND BASIC DEMOGRAPHICS

Shannon was a good, reliable designer—two qualities that likely would have allowed her to be moderately successful in the freelance business. But her side hustle really took off when she focused more intently on whom she hoped to serve. Once she realized she had a clear idea of someone—and that person was "just like her"—she began to see much more income coming in, especially as she created courses and products that didn't take as much time as full-on design work.

You're probably familiar with demographic data, which refers to simple categories like gender, age, education level, and so on. These factors aren't completely irrelevant in understanding your target customer, and depending on your offer, they may be particularly important. If you're selling SAT test prep coaching, you want to market to college-bound high school students. If your service helps men create better online dating profiles, you should craft the offer language to appeal entirely to men.

Sometimes it's not so simple, though. Many products and services cross demographic lines and are enjoyed by people from a variety of backgrounds. Creating an avatar—that single, specific, imaginary person—allows you to dig deeper and get much more precise about whom you're planning to serve.

Shannon started her Wordpress teaching business after becoming dissatisfied with on-the-side client work. She carefully considered her market and redesigned the whole operation around people just like her.

John Lee developed his podcast by thinking long and hard about "Jimmy," his imaginary listener who was disenchanted with work and longed for something greater.

Who will your side hustle serve? Who is that one person who *must* have what you're offering? Start with that person, take him or her out on an imaginary coffee date, and keep them in mind as your side hustle develops. Your success—and maybe theirs, too—depends on it.

Transform Your Idea into an Offer

Once you have a great idea and an ideal customer, you need to transform the idea into an offer. An offer has a promise, a pitch, and a price.

Jake Posko worked in higher education, managing a team and representing his university at local events. On the side he played guitar and sang with a small band, mostly for fun but occasionally for hire at weddings and events. He'd pursued a few different hustles in recent years, some of which had fallen flat and others that had been moderately successful.

One day he decided to try bringing in another stream of income by offering guitar lessons. If you think this isn't a terribly original idea, you're right. Here's the thing about playing guitar: lots of people already know how to play a few chords, and they're not necessarily looking to advance their skills. At the same time, plenty of other people offer lessons of varying expense and quality. In other words, there's not a ton of demand, *and* it's a crowded market.

Jake knew he had to stand out somehow. But upon doing a bit of detective work, the kind you learned about on Day 7, he realized that even though plenty of people offer guitar lessons, most of them don't put much care into their ads. "Guitar teacher for hire" is a pretty common headline—accurate, but hardly exciting.

Jake's first ad, which he posted on Craigslist, made a bold claim:

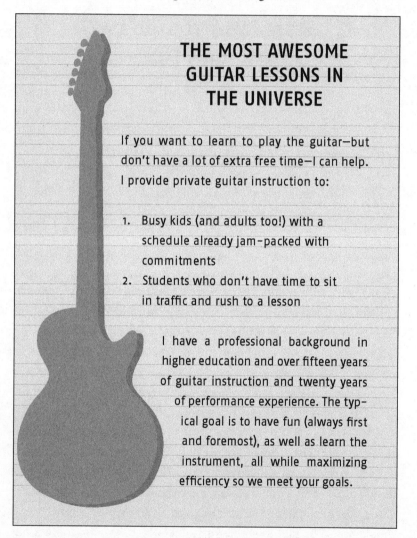

THE MOST AWESOME GUITAR LESSONS IN THE UNIVERSE

If you want to learn to play the guitar—but don't have a lot of extra free time—I can help. I provide private guitar instruction to:

1. Busy kids (and adults too!) with a schedule already jam-packed with commitments
2. Students who don't have time to sit in traffic and rush to a lesson

I have a professional background in higher education and over fifteen years of guitar instruction and twenty years of performance experience. The typical goal is to have fun (always first and foremost), as well as learn the instrument, all while maximizing efficiency so we meet your goals.

"Most awesome guitar lessons in the universe" sounds a lot better than "guitar teacher for hire." Even if the claim is a bit of a stretch, it's funny and gets people's attention right away. Still, as awesome as Jake's guitar lessons promised to be, he didn't have customers breaking down the door right away. It took some time before his first student booked a lesson, but he kept at it, working on the hustle during most of his limited free time over the next eight months.

Recognizing that his bold ad was probably the best tool he had at his disposal for getting the attention of potential customers, he decided to expand its reach, running ads on Google with similar language about why his lessons were so spectacular. Less than a year later, he was regularly earning $80 an hour for lessons and decided to quit his job to focus on further growing his side hustle.*

FROM IDEA TO OFFER

To have a real-world side hustle, you need to transform your idea into an offer. At a bare minimum, an offer tells people exactly what they will get for their money—and it also usually makes clear how much money is required to get it. "Guitar lessons" is not an offer. "Hour-long guitar lessons for $50" is getting closer, but even better yet would be something like:

> *"Learn guitar basics quickly (and have fun doing it) from a veteran instructor with twenty years of performance experience. To sign up for hour-long lessons at $50 a lesson, call 555-Hot-Tunes now."*

When you're presenting an offer, you want to make sure to give people all the pertinent information they need to make a purchase. A complete offer includes the following elements.

---

* Jake started the hustle while working a full-time job with a nine-month-old at home and a wife who also worked and went to school full-time. "There's no perfect time to start," he told me. "Just start."

THE PROMISE: how your hustle will change someone's life
THE PITCH: why they should purchase or sign up *now*
THE PRICE: what it costs to purchase or sign up (and how to
do it)

The *promise* should focus on the benefit people will receive from whatever you're selling. You want to craft a short, bold statement that attracts attention and makes the benefit to customers immediately clear. "The most awesome guitar lessons in the universe" is a great promise that illustrates this concept well.

The *pitch* should provide everything someone needs to know, without getting bogged down in a bunch of irrelevant details. A key part of the pitch is urgency, which is related to the concept of persuasiveness you learned about on Day 2. A bold, flashy offer is a great start, but for best results, you need to also provide a persuasive answer to this all-important question: Why should they take action *right now*?

The *price* should tell prospective customers or clients not only what your product or service costs, but also what it includes and exactly what they need to do to receive it. This last part is also known as a *call to action*. Examples include: click this button, call this number, sign up here, and so on. It should be easy and obvious.

Once more, consider a few of the ideas you've read about so far—and now see how they might have morphed from idea into offer.

IDEA: Curriculum Guides (Day 6)
OFFER: "You'll love this detailed curriculum guide that covers the North American geography material for fifth grade. The guide includes over thirty-five pages of information. I've also included a checklist for showing students how to create their class projects, including

guiding questions that will make writing it really straightforward. You'll get all this for just $20."

IDEA: Database lessons (Day 3)
OFFER: "Take a private lesson on using Microsoft Access to save time and be more productive. Sessions are $55 an hour online and $65 in person. Spots are filling up—reserve yours online at DatabasePro.com."

IDEA: Make your own liquor (Day 4)
OFFER: "Want to impress your guests with fancy homemade cocktails? Buy our Homemade Gin Kit ($49.95) and make gin in your bathtub . . . or maybe just your freezer. Get yours before Prohibition returns."

That's the basic idea. Before going any further, see if you can shift your idea into a simple (yet specific) offer.

Your Idea: _____

Your Promise: _____

Your Pitch: _____

Your Call to Action: _____

Now put it all together in a couple of brief and catchy lines:

Your Offer: _____

_____

_____

_____

_____

_____.

FIVE WAYS TO CREATE URGENCY

A successful offer doesn't just show people why they need what you are selling; it also shows them why they need it *now*. Here are a few tips to ensure that your call to action feels as urgent as possible.

1. Use words like *now* and *today* in your call to action. Even if the offer will never change and never sell out, urgent language will spur your customers into action.

2. If you want your customers to act quickly ("purchase now"), you should act quickly too. When you get customer inquiries, respond as fast as you can. A study by the *Harvard Business Review* showed that when companies replied within one hour of the customer's initial request for information, they were seven times more likely to sell to them.

3. When we talk about testing on Day 20, you'll learn that little details like the specific colors you use on your website or in your marketing aren't that important. There's one exception: use red for text meant to communicate urgency, especially when showing a discount or other time-sensitive call to action.

4. Announce an upcoming price increase, but give people enough time to make a purchase or commitment before the change goes into effect ($19.97 this week only!). This is essentially another way to have a sale without calling it a sale.

5. If selling online, add a countdown timer to your checkout page ("Time left to purchase: 3 hours, 14 minutes, 3 seconds . . .") There's no rule that says you can't start the timer over again once it reaches the end of the clock.

"SIMPLE COPYWRITING STUFF"

Jake called his ad strategy "just simple copywriting 101 stuff," and technically he was right—he wasn't the first side hustler to use superlatives ("most awesome lessons in the universe") or to offer a strong promise. Still, it worked because so few other people in his market were thinking that way.

As Jake discovered, wording your offer in a way that makes it sound even just a bit more compelling than your competition's can give you a real edge. You don't learn this type of writing in school, but with a bit of practice, it's not too hard a skill to pick up.

- Write to a person, not a group. Remember the ideal customer from Day 8: talk directly to that person and pretend there is no one else in the world.

- Have a purpose for every word. In good copywriting, nothing is superfluous. Every fact and every bullet point is there for a reason. Write multiple drafts and edit ruthlessly each time.

- Use numbers. There's a very good reason so many headlines include numbers: they get our attention faster than words. That principle doesn't just apply to headlines; use numbers throughout your pitch. How awesome are the most awesome guitar lessons in the universe? They're approximately 36 percent more awesome than the second-most awesome lessons!

- Use words that elicit joy, surprise, reassurance, and other positive emotions. Keep it fun and lively. Don't just list a bunch of features; maintain the focus on how your offer *makes people feel better in some way*.

- Help customers see themselves as part of the story. A good way to do this is through testimonials, which also provide social proof. Show potential buyers that there is someone else "just like them" who is thrilled with your offer.

- Use action verbs. The side hustler *launched* her offer. The customer *placed* an order right away. The side hustler *rejoiced*.

- Show excitement! You *believe* in your offer. You *know* it's going to improve people's lives in some meaningful way. Enthusiasm is contagious, so don't be afraid to put yours on display.

Keep it pithy, but be sure not to leave out any information that might persuade your potential buyer. Always keep the three elements in mind: promise, pitch, and a price.

Jake Posko started out by charging $50 an hour for "the most awesome guitar lessons in the universe." He gradually raised his rates until he reached what he thought the market could handle, somewhere between $80 and $120 an hour depending on the location of the lesson and how many lessons people paid for in advance. His first month, he earned $420. His second month, he earned $1,535. Just six months later, he was taking in $2,800 in a single month and was ready to quit his job—which he did.

He now sees take-home pay of around $5,000 to $6,000 a month, working twenty to twenty-five hours a week. With steady clients and continued referrals, the side hustle is now a primary income earner that allows him to spend more time at home with his wife and young child. It was, in a word, *awesome*.

Create Your Origins Story

> Like a comic book superhero, your side hustle needs a history. Don't just give 'em the facts; tell them a story.

David Venn, a Canadian, found love in Amsterdam when he met Praj, who is originally from Kathmandu, Nepal. Did you get all that? In any case, they got engaged and wanted to get married in a traditional ceremony back in Praj's homeland. The trip was David's first to Nepal, and he loved everything about the country—the people, of course, but also the art and in particular the fashion. The chilly Himalayan mountain ranges are the source of much of the world's supply of cashmere, and the production of luxurious sweaters and scarves has been a hallmark of Nepalese culture for generations.

After honeymooning in Nepal, the couple planned to settle in Canada, another land known for its frigid winters. David had noticed that cashmere products in Nepal were much cheaper than anywhere else he'd seen. He wondered if there might be a market for those products in his own wintery homeland. Despite the high cost, cashmere was popular in Canada, so he knew he wouldn't have to spend much time explaining to people what it was. A side hustle idea was born!

The next few weeks were a blur, as David and Praj met with dozens of local suppliers in search of a partner. Eventually they discovered one who shared their commitment to making high-quality accessories with care and attention to detail. They started with an order of one hundred women's shawls, spending about $2,000 to acquire and import them to Canada.

Corala Cashmere launched just in time for the holiday season. After garnering a feature in the fashion section of their citywide newspaper, the newlywed hustlers sold out all hundred shawls, netting a tidy $3,000 profit that they mostly invested back into the business. Making money was great, but they weren't the only ones reaping the benefits: from the beginning, they had intended for Corala Cashmere to give back to the communities where the materials were produced. Praj knew that many mountain shepherds in Nepal lacked the resources to pay for their children's education, a problem that impacts girls disproportionately. So they immediately sent back 5 percent of the profits to a local charity, along with another order that allowed them to continue building their hustle.

DON'T JUST GIVE 'EM THE FACTS, TELL THEM A STORY

Like every story in this book, the story of Corala Cashmere is true. Imagine, however, if I'd told you a different version: David and Praj wanted to make some extra cash, so they decided to import cashmere shawls from Nepal and resell them for a profit back in David's native Canada. *Cha-ching!*

What's the problem with that story? It's factually correct, and there's certainly nothing wrong with making money (that's why you're reading this book!). On its own, however, that story is *boring*. There's no depth to it, and not much of a hook to grab or inspire the reader . . . or a potential customer.

Now consider the details in the first story:

- David and Praj fell in love and traveled to her native country for their wedding.

- The idea to start a business came to them as they explored Nepal and talked with local suppliers.

- Corala Cashmere benefits schoolchildren in the Himalayan mountains; customers can feel good about their purchase because they know it's responsibly sourced and a portion of profits goes back to the community.

Remember how that first order of one hundred shawls sold out in large part because of the media feature they received? Without the backstory, it's much less likely that the newspaper would have written about them—and it's much less likely that people would care. That's because the story of Corala Cashmere is a great *origins story*: a compelling and inspiring narrative of the *why* behind their side hustle. No matter what it is you're selling, you need an origins story, too.

BE THE SUPERHERO OF YOUR ORIGINS STORY

The phrase "origins story" comes from the world of comic books, whose artists construct histories of how superheroes or villains gain their powers and turn into the unique characters they're known for. A good origins story usually features a turning point or moment of transformation in which the character evolves in a significant way or receives a mission he must complete. Unless you're selling a completely generic product (and you probably shouldn't be), you'll be much more successful if you provide your customers with a history about how your hustle came to be.

Even if your side hustle origins don't involve falling in love in

Amsterdam or honeymooning in Nepal, there's still a story in it somewhere. Think back about what got you into this—why were you interested in starting a side hustle in the first place? Then, when you found an idea, where did the inspiration come from? If you had more than one idea, why did you select that one?

Consider, in brief, the origins stories of a couple of hustles you've read about so far in the book:

- When an animal lover misses her family pets after moving to Texas from Spain, she finds a way to enjoy the company of a different furry companion every day—while providing a useful service for traveling pet owners—when she starts an "Airbnb for dogs" in her home.

- A specialized teacher with a love for curriculum finds a way to help her colleagues spend less time on lesson planning and more time with students by designing customized teaching resources.

Big businesses know all about origins stories, or at least they think they do. Billion-dollar insurance companies are eager to tell you heartwarming, humble histories about how they've been providing families with financial security "from generation to generation"—that is, at least as long as you pay your premiums and don't file many claims. A big-box retailer with thousands of stores will play up its modest "mom-and-pop shop" beginnings as much as possible, all in an attempt to be seen as a scrappy underdog rather than a giant corporation.

Those giant corporations have some real business advantages, from scale to tax codes, but don't worry: this is an area where *your side hustle has an edge*. A multinational corporation may *try* to tell a humble origins story, but if authenticity is what you're after, it's hard to beat a typical side hustler's story. Side hustlers don't have to work hard to be humble—we already are! You're better than a multinational corporation that pretends to be "just like" their millions of customers. You have a *real* origins story, and you are the hero of it.

This brings up a good point. Unless you have a reason to not include any information about yourself in the origins story, it's almost always a good idea to infuse some personality into your narrative. After all, you're not creating a massive corporation (at least not at the moment)—you're building something for yourself, by yourself. You *are* the side hustle story, so if there's a random fact about why you love your hustle, include it! These facts are not irrelevant to your mission; in fact, they're essential.

Personal details will also help you forge an emotional connection with your ideal customer. Remember Shannon Mattern, the IT director from Day 8, whose hustle took off once she realized she was her own ideal customer? Her website lists her professional qualifications and showcases her portfolio, of course—but that's not all. On the well-designed About page, you can learn all sorts of other facts about her, including her favorite Taylor Swift song, how she goes to the gym to work off her weekend Miller Lite indulgence, and how she felt when she got her first client. As an outsider, you may think, *Whoa, too much information . . . who cares about this stuff?* But that's exactly the point: *not everyone cares, but her ideal customers do.* Those customers are just like her, and this approach helps them relate to her on a more personal level.

SIDE HUSTLE STORIES: FILL IN THE BLANKS

To create your origins story, first consider *why* you're pursuing this particular hustle in the first place. Of all the ideas you could have chosen, what was compelling, special, or just interesting about this one? These prompts may help:

I've always been interested in _____

_____,

so I decided to try _____

_____

_____.

I was frustrated by _____

_____

and knew there was a better way. I made _____

_____

to help other people with the same problem.

I started this hustle because I noticed _____

_____.

There didn't seem to be anyone else doing anything about it (or the existing businesses were missing something important), so I made _____

_____

_____.

Loosely using this formula, here's how a couple of other ~~people~~ superheroes in the book might describe their origins stories:

> "I went on a cruise and was frustrated that I couldn't find answers to some simple questions before I left. I started a blog to help other people with the same problem. It now brings in more than $4,000 each month."
> —TANNER CALLAIS, CRUZELY [DAY 13]

"Like more than 300,000 other people in the Bay Area, every day I commuted to work. At the time there was no smartphone app that combined traffic and public transit data into a single stream of info, so I created it. It's now used by more than 40,000 people every day."

—STEVEN PETERSON, ROUTESY [DAY 17]

Back in Canada, Corala Cashmere was taking off. After a slight rebranding (the original name was Karma Cashmere), David and Praj began to add new designs and colors. Their long-term vision is for at least one of them to work on it full-time. For now, though, it continues to grow organically, with almost all sales coming through search results and referrals.

As we see from this story, the more you can inspire your potential customers to root for you and your mission, the easier it will be to turn potential customers into paying ones. Dig deep to find that story, and don't be afraid to share it widely as you develop your hustle.

WEEK 2 RECAP!

You learned how to generate side hustle ideas (remember, they're everywhere!) and how to select from a multitude of different options. You've figured out who your ideal customer is and crafted an origins story sure to inspire. And finally, you've turned your hustle idea into a full-fledged offer. In the next section, we'll be diving right in to do everything we need to get your offer up and running. Forward motion!

— **KEY POINTS** —

- Some ideas are better than others. Use the Side Hustle Selector to find the best ones by comparing them on a range of criteria.

- You don't have to be better than the competition in every way, but you should at least be *different*. Become a detective and survey the landscape to understand what else is out there.

- Get super clear on your avatar or ideal customer. Start with the basics, but then think about some deeper questions: What do they really want? What are their hopes and dreams? These answers will guide you as you prepare to launch with maximum impact.

WEEK 2: SELECT YOUR BEST IDEA

Day 6:	Use the Side Hustle Selector to Compare Ideas	✓
Day 7:	Become a Detective	✓
Day 8:	Have Imaginary Coffee with Your Ideal Customer	✓
Day 9:	Transform Your Idea Into an Offer	✓
Day 10:	Create Your Origins Story	✓

WEEK 3

PREPARE FOR LIFTOFF

You've settled on your idea. This week you'll learn how to quickly implement it, without getting bogged down in unimportant details.

WEEK 3: PREPARE FOR LIFTOFF

Day 11: Assemble the Nuts and Bolts

Day 12: Decide How to Price Your Offer

Day 13: Create a Side Hustle Shopping List

Day 14: Set up a Way to Get Paid

Day 15: Design Your First Workflow

Day 16: Spend 10% More Time on the Most Important Tasks

Assemble the Nuts and Bolts

> Resourcefulness is your most valuable skill as a side hustler. Get a head start on sourcing everything you'll need to launch your project sooner rather than later.

If you can't find what you're looking for, make it for yourself and anyone else who might want it. This classic business lesson led Sarah Hannington to a six-figure side hustle. In her case, she was looking for custom-printed candy hearts to send to clients at her marketing day job. It sounded like a fun idea for a Valentine's Day–themed gift, and surely it couldn't be hard to find . . . right?

Sarah searched high and low, but no one seemed to be offering exactly what she had in mind. In desperation, she started contacting candy manufacturers. One of them replied on Facebook Messenger to say that they offered the service, and at a reasonable price.

When she looked for details about that manufacturer online, however, she came up empty-handed. The company's website contained almost no information on what they did and how customers could place an order. Sarah wrote back to the company and explained that she worked in marketing and could help them shore up their online presence, but they didn't even acknowledge the offer. When she finally spoke to a sales rep on the phone, he didn't know anything about the website and seemed generally unenthusiastic. He did, however, offer to fulfill any orders she sent.

As a marketer, Sarah took their lack of response as a challenge. True, she didn't know anything about the candy business, and she didn't have much experience as an entrepreneur. But she knew marketing, so she decided to put those skills to work. Valentine's Day was approaching, so she quickly built a three-page website using a template and advertised custom-printed candy hearts at a higher price than what the unresponsive manufacturer charged. Since no one else was competing for this space, within a matter of days her site was number one in Google search results. That same day, she got her first order—then three more in quick succession.

Within two weeks, orders were arriving every day. Even though she was only reselling, meaning that all she had to do was transmit the orders to that lethargic manufacturer and track deliveries, the volume of orders was overwhelming and she struggled to keep up. And it wasn't just her: the manufacturer also fell behind. During peak order time, the unenthusiastic sales rep sent her an email explaining that they couldn't keep up and wouldn't be able to fulfill all the orders by the holiday. *Womp-womp.*

Custom-printed candy hearts is a seasonal business, with 90 percent of orders coming in during the six to eight weeks before Valentine's Day. For the following year's season, Sarah was determined to avoid being dependent on an unreliable manufacturer. But what would she do? She was good at marketing but knew next to nothing about production lines and commercial printing equipment.

In what was quickly becoming a theme of this hustling experiment, Sarah decided to simply figure it out. A more extensive search led to a Chinese supplier, who claimed to have a machine that would do everything Sarah needed. Alas, when the machine arrived a month later, it didn't work. Undeterred, she started calling around to every company she could think of, large and small.

Five weeks before the Valentine's Day season began, she found one that promised to sell her equipment that actually worked. It cost her all of her revenue for that year, but this was a side hustle, not her primary source of income—and she knew if it worked out, she'd be much more prepared for next season.

Orders were already arriving, so Sarah was nervous. Thankfully, this new company came through: they delivered the custom-made machine on schedule, and best of all, it actually worked. To meet the huge demand, Sarah and a small team of assistants ran it twelve hours a day, seven days a week. She got it all done under the wire, sending the final orders via overnight courier to make sure that everyone received them in time. It was a ton of work, but now she was sitting in a good place for next year: she had the number one Google ranking for a product that lots of people clearly wanted, *and* the ability to fulfill all the orders herself.

EVERYTHING IS FIGUREOUTABLE

My friend Marie Forleo likes to say that everything is "figureoutable." This lesson is well illustrated throughout Sarah's story. She didn't know how to do half the things she needed to start this business, but along the way, she figured it out. When she encountered problems, she found a way to solve them. When she hit obstacles, she searched for a way around them.

PROBLEM: Can't locate custom-printed candy supplier online
SOLUTION: Ask candy manufacturers for referrals

PROBLEM: Too dependent on unreliable manufacturer
SOLUTION: Find a way to "DIY it" by taking production in-house

PROBLEM: First machine doesn't work (thanks, China)
SOLUTION: Invest entire season's revenue in new machine

Sarah is skilled at many things, but perhaps the most important of those skills is resourcefulness. She decided what she wanted to do, and then she found a way to make it happen.

Side hustlers are generally a resourceful bunch, and resourcefulness is often worth more than any amount of business experience or know-how. Don't know how to get a business license where you live? Go online and type in "business license" followed by your state, province, or country. Not sure how to file your side hustle income on your taxes? Schedule a thirty-minute call with an accountant.

The point is, where some people might see these things as obstacles, side hustlers know they are just details. They aren't that hard to figure out, and as Sarah's story shows, it's much better to spend your time on things that will help your hustle make money.

THE $100,000 STARTUP

Sarah's candy heart machine was custom made, and it didn't come cheap. As a rush, custom job, it cost her more than $100,000. Wait, aren't you supposed to be frugal when starting a side hustle? That machine was #@!% expensive! But take note: Sarah didn't spend that money until she had a proven model. Her *first* investment, building a quick-and-dirty website using an online template, cost almost nothing.

Only after she had received a lot of orders two seasons in a row (and only after other options proved futile) did she decide to buy her own equipment. By that point, her expected annual revenue exceeded the cost of the machine, so she was confident it was a safe bet. Plus, she knew that the next year her profit margins would be much higher, since she wouldn't have any expensive equipment to buy.

It doesn't *have* to take money to make money, but sometimes, big investments in a proven hustle can pay off.

THE MINI-TOOLKIT

After I wrote *The $100 Startup*, I went out on the road and did an extensive book tour. Along the way I was a guest on many different radio and TV shows, where people were invited to call in and ask questions about the nuts and bolts of bootstrapping a business. To my surprise, a great number of the questions from listeners and viewers related to taxes, business licenses, and minor administrative functions. Why was I surprised? Well, because in many cases, these questions were from people *who had no idea what their business was actually going to do or how it would make money.*

Asking, "Is this a feasible and profitable idea?" is a much more important question than "Which bookkeeping software should I use?" Logistical questions like these are all "figureoutable," but without a plan for generating income, you don't have a hustle.

Still, no matter how resourceful you are, it never hurts to start with a mini-toolkit—so here are some recommendations. These tips, based on my years of hustling and work with thousands of small-business owners, may help you make a few decisions. A quick disclaimer: your situation may vary, and none of this advice is likely to be universal. Still, these *general principles* will apply to many people and many different kinds of hustles.

1. Get a bank account that's just for your side hustle.
   There is little to no difference between what the bank calls "business" and "personal" accounts, so just get

the option that's easiest for you. The most important thing is to keep your funds separate.

2. Similarly, get a separate credit or debit card you use only for expenses associated with your hustle. Bonus tip: make sure you're earning airline miles for them!

3. Pay for everything you can up front. Not only will this prevent you from investing more than you can afford, paying up front instead of thirty or sixty days later feels good. You'll operate lean and worry far less if you don't owe money to anyone.

4. Set aside at least 25 percent of your hustle income for taxes. Again, your situation may vary—but unless you're exempt for some reason, don't forget to set aside money for your annual or quarterly donations to the government.

   Side note: Paying taxes on money you make is not a problem, it's a by-product of success. I once participated in a twenty-two-message email exchange with someone who was greatly upset about having to pay a supplemental tax of $100 on every $25,000 he made. This is hardly a cause for complaint! Be thankful that you've earned the money in the first place.

5. Be fast with invoicing. It's good to pay people quickly, but it's even better to *get* paid quickly. Don't save invoicing for one day at the end of the month. When you do the work or make the sale, send the bill.

6. Whenever possible, insist on a written agreement for service work. This doesn't need to be a dense, twenty-page contract drawn up by an expensive lawyer. You

just want to get the basic terms in writing to avoid any future disagreement or misunderstanding. See page 104 for a customizable email you can use as a basic agreement.

7. Legal structure: operating as a sole proprietor is perfectly acceptable for many hustles. If you need to incorporate your hustle, you can often do that yourself online for much less money than it would cost to hire an attorney. (Once more, your situation may vary.)

8. Right from the beginning, set up a very simple accounting system. This should be cheap or free and can grow with you if the hustle takes off, but do have a means of tracking income and expenses. See Day 23 for a couple of options.

9. If at all possible, set aside a dedicated hustle workspace, even a small one, in your home or apartment. If that's *not* possible, create a mobile one. For example, if you like to work at a coffee shop, go to the same one at the same time, and try to work from the same table. The idea is to create a pattern and a routine that will make it easier to work on the hustle consistently.

10. Once you're making money, pay yourself first. Set up a system to transfer profits from your hustle account to your personal account on a regular basis. Don't have it set to transfer continuously as sales come in (that can be very difficult to track or record later), but *do* withdraw at least some profits on a regular basis. Getting paid is empowering!

"GET IT IN WRITING?" YES, BUT IT'S EASY

Don't be intimidated by the word *contract*. If you're freelancing or otherwise doing contract work with clients, you should absolutely have some sort of written agreement, but it doesn't necessarily need to be a hefty document with lots of fine print. The most important thing is to have clear communication regarding the work to be completed, a timeline by which it will be done, and the fee you'll be paid.

In lieu of a formal contract, after you get off the phone with a new client who's just agreed to hire you, you might send a quick email like this:

> *"Hey, Paul, thanks for the chat! To recap, we agreed that I'd visit your workplace once a month for the next three months to assist with improving the interior design and office layout. My fee for this work (including a detailed report and any reasonable follow-up communication) is $1,500. You'll pay 50% now and the other 50% after you receive the detailed report. Is that all correct? If so, I'll send an invoice for the first 50% so I can get started right away!"*

An email like that summarizes all the important factors without getting bogged down in excessive details. If anything ever goes wrong, or if the client expects additional work without additional pay, you can quickly refer back to this communication.

Sarah kept her day job even as the candy heart hustle became a sustainable, six-figure business. Because most orders arrived around Valentine's Day, the schedule was predictable and it didn't take a ton of time the rest of the year. In addition to the added stream of income, her experience produced yet another important benefit of starting your own project: her boss knows that she comes to work because she *wants* to, not because she has to. This led to a higher salary, as well as more recognition of Sarah's skills and value.

If you don't go to work because you want to, you need your own *sweet* success story, just like Sarah's. The story begins once you start earning money from something you really care about.

Decide How to Price Your Offer

> Pricing can be a challenge even for experienced hustlers. Use the cost-plus model and follow two simple guidelines to be way ahead of the curve.

Sara Everett has at least two professional identities. She's a construction project manager, and she's also an artist. In the first role, she coordinates with developers, architects, and planning teams for new apartment buildings in Seattle. Managing big building projects with lots of variables is complex, but Sara enjoys problem solving and helping people find collaborative solutions to challenges.

As someone with a strong artistic sensibility, she found herself troubled by something she noticed each time she walked through the communal areas of a new building. There were always prints hanging on the walls, but they were boring and lacked originality. They looked like the kind of mass-produced posters you'd buy when furnishing a dorm room or first apartment on a budget. As an artist, Sara saw an opportunity. Most real estate developers in her area didn't know a lot about art, and their impression was that "real" art was expensive. Of course, the kind of paintings that hang in museums or in the homes of billionaires *are* pricey, but Sara knew that works of art don't need to cost millions of dollars to have real artistic value.

From her involvement in the local arts community, Sara knew a number of great artists who would be thrilled to provide original artwork at a price that was fair to them but not out of reach for the building's budget. The artists and developers just needed a matchmaker, and she was perfect for the job: no one else knew so much about both the real estate world and the local community of working artists. These worlds conveniently overlapped in a major city, but no one had connected them.

Her first project was an original art program for a new building, an ambitious project that required a lot of work. At the time, not many developers in the Seattle market had attempted to place so much original artwork in one location. It was also a brand-new concept, both for Sara and for the developer. When the time came to discuss a fee, she wasn't sure what to suggest. She finally proposed $12,000, paid in monthly installments of $1,000 for a year. It was admittedly an imprecise figure, based somewhat arbitrarily on how much time she expected it to take.

The program was a huge success. Residents frequently praised the artwork, highlighting its role in fostering a much more authentic sense of community in the building. The only downside was that Sara had spent a lot more time working on it than she'd planned. At first she was thrilled to be paid an extra $1,000 a month for doing something she enjoyed, but by the time she finished and tallied up her hours she realized how much she'd underestimated and thus underbilled for her time.

No regrets, she thought; it had been a great learning experience. For the second time around, she proposed an hourly rate instead of a flat fee. She provided an estimate of the hours she expected to spend, with the understanding that she'd check in with the client if the project took longer than planned. This gave her the security of making a good hourly rate, all while still earning a regular salary from her day job.

HOW TO PRICE YOUR OFFER

On Day 9, you learned how to turn ideas into offers. You learned that a hustle is not complete without an offer, and an offer includes a price. The price may be variable, or it may be negotiable—but without at least some idea of what you'll charge for your offer, you have a hobby, not a hustle.

On Day 7 you learned how to be a side hustle detective and scope out the competitive landscape to see what others are charging for products or services similar to yours. But if your hustle is something that no one has really ever tried before, how are you supposed to know what your offer is worth—or more important, what customers will pay for it?

The first thing to know is there there's usually a range of possible prices you could successfully charge. You want it to be low enough that you don't turn away or lose customers, but high enough that you can still make money. Assuming you want to maximize profit, your long-term goal is to find a sweet spot at the higher end of what people are willing to pay.

That's the long-term goal. When you're getting started, however, you just want to make sure your price is high enough to make the project worthwhile for you. There's a simple model called "cost-plus" you can use to determine how to achieve that short-term goal. It differs a bit depending on if you're selling a product or a service, so let's break it down each way.

1. SELLING A PRODUCT

With cost-plus pricing applied to a product, you first figure out how much it will cost to provide the product, and then you simply add on a markup (a dollar amount or a percentage) that serves as your profit. How much should you add? Ah, that's the magic question—and the answer is different for everyone. To start with, consider how much income per sale would make that sale worthwhile to *you*, considering your costs as well as the time you'll spend developing the product.

You should also think about your *projected volume*: whether you hope to sell a small number of products (low volume), or a larger number (high volume). For higher volume products, you can charge a price just slightly above cost and still make a profit, but for lower volume products, your margin will need to be much higher.

Even so, minimum acceptable profit can vary widely from person to person, and it has as much to do with the goals you set for yourself on Day 1 as it does the specific nature of your hustle. On Day 6, you met Meredith Floyd-Preston, who sold curriculum guides for fellow Waldorf teachers. She deliberately set a low price for her guides, usually in the $8 to $20 range. This pricing was fine for her—once the guides were made, they cost very little to sell and distribute—and she was happy to be able to serve teachers who were on a budget. On the other hand, Andrew Church, who you'll read about on Day 21, creates hand-carved slate artwork. There are more hard costs and labor involved in making each piece, so some of his work costs $175 or more. In each example, both Meredith and Andrew considered both their costs *and* the income they wanted to make from their hustle.

2. SELLING A SERVICE

If you're providing a service, like Sara does for real estate developers, there aren't many hard expenses associated with the work. Naturally, this doesn't mean that she should charge a low price. Her clients pay for her skill and expertise, as well as the time she spends on all the tasks she needs to complete to make her projects successful.

To set an introductory price for a new service, start by deciding on your minimum acceptable hourly income. When you make this decision, don't consider only the time that is spent actually providing the service; be sure you consider any needed prep time or "lost" time that you'll spend on the work that won't go onto an invoice. When Sara thought hard about everything that would be involved, she decided that $100 an hour was the right price for her work. That's what she proposed to the real estate developers who eventually became her clients, and they agreed.

One good rule of thumb is that your minimum accepted hourly income should be at least what you make per hour in your day job, and probably more. Since you'll be working on the project in your spare time, the income you earn needs to be worth the leisure time you'll be giving up.

Ideally, you won't make *only* your minimum acceptable hourly income—you'll make more! But if you set that number as a floor, the lowest that you'll accept, you have a baseline from which to build. And if you can't make the hustle work at that minimum standard, that's a good sign that you need a new hustle.

To recap, just keep this in mind as you go along:

PRODUCT: Minimum acceptable profit per item or per sale
SERVICE: Minimum acceptable hourly income or flat rate

Sara found that there was an advantage for her in charging hourly. When she charged the flat rate on her first project, she made far less than the $100-an-hour rate she billed for the second one. However, a flat rate can have a major benefit, too: if you learn to work faster as you improve in providing the service, you'll be rewarded, not penalized. Sometimes you'll have to experiment a little to discover the best possible price for your offers.

DECIDE HOW TO PRICE YOUR OFFER   111

IF YOU'RE JUST "BREAKING EVEN," YOU'RE ACTUALLY LOSING MONEY

A side hustle should be fun, but as you know by now, it also needs to be profitable. Consider the platform Fiverr.com, which we'll look at further in a couple of upcoming stories. This online marketplace for services and others like it (TaskRabbit, for example) are great for experimenting in the way of the side hustle: you can create a profile and start completing tasks for people almost right away. What's not to love? Well, the site is called *Fiverr* for a reason—the price for all the services offered needs to begin at just $5. It's possible to use the platform as a launchpad for working up to something bigger, and it's also totally fine to play around at a low price structure while getting used to hustling, but in the long run you'll probably want to make a lot more than $5 at a time.

For various reasons, corporations sometimes accept breaking even on a project, or even taking a loss in order to gain something else. But a side hustle doesn't have shareholders or other profit centers to pick up the slack. If you spend twenty hours a week working on your hustle and all it does is break even, you've actually *lost* money because your time is worth a lot more than $0. Profit *must* be built into the hustle from the beginning.

The great thing about side hustles is that you can set your hustle's price *based on what works for you*. With this method of pricing, you determine your desired profit, then you examine what needs to happen to achieve the goal. If you exceed the goal, that's awesome! Think of that goal as your *minimum standard of success*. Anything better than that is even more validation of your winning idea, and even more money in the bank.

FOLLOW THESE PRICING POINTERS TO THE BANK

Pricing is both an art and a science. On Day 20, you'll learn about A/B testing, where you can offer multiple prices and see how it affects conversion rates. That's the scientific method—for a more creative one, consider these guidelines.

1. Whenever possible, design your hustle with recurring revenue in mind. Why sell something once when you can sell it over and over? Recurring revenue isn't possible in every hustle, but it's a worthwhile point of consideration when comparing different ideas. If all other factors are equal and one idea offers the potential for recurring revenue—like a monthly membership, or regular, paid upgrades, that idea is likely your winner.

2. Consider offering pricing tiers, where customers can pay more to get more. It's good to give people *some* amount of choice, but not too much. Have you ever been to a restaurant that has 150 different items on the menu, or one that offers many different types of cuisines? If you haven't, you're not missing much—it's hard to make decisions about what to order, and the food at such places is rarely good. The same goes for creating offers. When it comes to pricing options, two or three choices is usually enough.

3. Be careful of being too clever, and leave the gimmicks to the home shopping networks. A seemingly clever "pay what you will" fad recently swept the world of online courses and e-books. This is not usually a good idea—it confuses your customers, and most will end up paying less than

they would if you simply took the time to find the optimal price. Instead of having clever pricing, have a great product and a fair (fixed) price.

4. Don't stray too far from market prices. Remember how Jake Posko, the guitar teacher, started out at $50 an hour and eventually moved to $80–$120 an hour. You may wonder why he didn't keep moving it even higher. Well, as he experimented with different prices, Jake discovered that there was a natural ceiling for his new profession. No matter how awesome his "most awesome guitar lessons in the universe" were, $80–$120 was the highest acceptable range for guitar lessons in general. If he priced any *higher*, he'd lose clients. If he priced much *lower*, he'd lose money. After all, if you could keep increasing a price forever without customers dropping off, we'd all be running our side hustles from a mansion in Beverly Hills.

HOW DOES THIS PRICE MAKE YOU FEEL?

"How do I decide how much to sell something for? I think about how it makes me feel." I was first introduced to this concept by Danielle LaPorte, a longtime friend from Vancouver, Canada, who makes goal-setting calendars, custom jewelry, and other items in addition to being a bestselling author. I have to admit that when she said this, I didn't get it at all. "What do you mean, how it makes you *feel*?" I asked.

She explained that whenever she's trying to decide the final price for a new product, she focuses on the feeling she gets when she thinks about a particular number being out in the world. Then, she selects the final price.

This approach may sound a little "out there," but here's the thing: Danielle doesn't have these feelings in a complete void of information. She's an experienced entrepreneur who's started and ran several successful companies—and it's that experience that gives her the intuition to guide her pricing choices.

As time went by I thought about this concept more and more. When I make pricing decisions now, I usually complete the process by asking myself the same question. It doesn't always give me all the information I need, but it can often confirm if I'm on the right track.

Sara, the construction project manager who doubles as an art consultant, has now completed ten building projects. The hourly pricing model she switched to continues to work well for her and her clients. Last year, some friends were getting together to see a play in London and invited her to come along. In her pre-hustle days, Sara would never have had the budget for such an extravagance, but this time, when they said, "It would be fun if you could come!" Sara replied, "Why not?" and then purchased a flight from Seattle to Heathrow. She used her side hustle money to take the spontaneous trip, feeling justified rather than stressed about the expense. She had worked hard for this money, and she deserved the reward.

Like Sara, you may need to adjust your pricing model as you discover how it works in the real world. But remember, you still must set a price, and you still must show a profit. Establish your minimum price, work toward getting to the sweet spot (in Jake's story, $80 an hour is a lot better than $50 an hour), and experiment with different options. Only by publishing your offer and seeing how customers react will you know if your price is viable.

Create a Side Hustle Shopping List

Your hustle will probably require specific tools, resources, and deliverables. Learn to find, gather, or create everything on your shopping list.

In the fall of 2015, Tanner Callais and his wife received a wedding present in the form of a gift certificate for a cruise vacation. Neither of them had been on a cruise before, and they weren't particularly excited about it—but they went anyway and ended up having a great time.

Part of their initial hesitancy was that they couldn't find much information online about the cruising experience. Sure, there was a detailed cruise line website, but that consisted mostly of promotional material. They wanted to know what it was *really* like. They also found a bunch of forums where veteran cruisers swapped recommendations and experiences, but those presented another problem: with thousands of opinions, it was only natural that many of them contradicted one another. Tanner didn't want to wade through a multitude of forum threads where cruisers argued over which lobster dinner was best; he just needed some basic, unbiased info to help him lower his costs and have a better experience.

The lack of impartial, accessible information inspired him to do something to fill the gap. As a full-time copywriter for his day job, he already knew how to instill information in a helpful, yet entertaining way. So upon his return from the high seas, he set out to build the website that he himself had wanted to consult before he'd set off.

The first thing he did was simply write. Tanner opened up a blank document on his laptop and began to jot down all sorts of ideas for articles. He wasn't concerned with all the details at first; he simply wanted to have a substantial number of article topics that he could use to fill out the site when he launched it.

Then, after slapping together a quick website, he shifted his focus to search-engine optimization, also known as SEO. His goal was to spend $0 on marketing, and devote all promotional efforts toward getting ranked high in Google and other search engines for terms and phrases that new cruisers were likely to search for. Since he himself had been a new cruiser with lots of questions he couldn't find answers for, he knew what information people wanted, and what terms they might search for.

Here's an example: before he left for the cruise, Tanner wondered if he'd be able to watch Netflix while on board. Tens of millions of people subscribe to Netflix, and presumably many of them go on cruises—but Tanner couldn't find anyone who'd answered this question succinctly. Therefore, one of his articles on the new site was called "Answered: Can I watch Netflix on a cruise?"

After posting the article, the page jumped to the top few Google search results, and he immediately began seeing more traffic on the site. He applied this strategy over and over, answering questions that were commonly asked (yet not commonly answered) by curious cruisers.

This wasn't a hobby; it was a hustle. To make money, Tanner added advertising and affiliate programs to the new site. That way, he'd get paid when visitors clicked on the ads or joined a program he linked to. He was excited when his new site brought in $100 a month, but he didn't stop there. He kept adding pages, answering questions, and optimizing for Google. In less than a year, the side hustle was making more than $3,000 a month.

THE RECIPE FOR HUSTLING SUCCESS

At this point you've settled on a hustle idea, turned that idea into an offer, and decided how much you're going to charge for that offer. You're just about ready to launch! But every side hustle requires some setup work: a list of things you need to either source, acquire, or prepare to bring your offer into the world.

The beauty of Tanner's idea for a blog about cruises lies both in its simplicity and its execution. Sure, it was a great idea—but as you know by now, a lot of great ideas don't necessarily translate to feasible and profitable side hustles. This one was great *yet simple to implement.* Because side hustles are designed to be moneymaking projects that you can get off the ground quickly, you want to be able to design a simple and efficient process to go from idea to implementation in as little time as possible.

Imagine that you decide to make a little extra cash by selling fresh bread at a local bake sale, and imagine that you've never baked bread before. Maybe you have skills at the level of Martha Stewart or Rachael Ray in the kitchen, but for the purpose of this example, pretend that you're like me: you're pretty good at boiling water and pouring it on coffee beans. Once in a while, you might even be able to toast a bagel. Otherwise, your skills are restricted to visiting bakeries and calling for delivery.

In this scenario, you have to bake the bread from scratch—no ordering out. There are a couple of ways to approach this project. You could take a deep dive into the annals of bread history, camping out in the library to read up on the science of bread making. You could arrange visits to half a dozen bakeries to interview master bakers, comparing their answers on the ratio of flour to water, preferred oven temperature, and so on.

Or you could skip all that, and simply get to work. In the fast-track baking plan, you'd look online for a recipe that provided simple instructions, and you could probably find one in thirty seconds or less. Without going to great effort, your tasks would be:

1. Find a good recipe

2. Gather the necessary ingredients

3. Follow the recipe step by step

By completing these simple steps, most likely you'd accomplish your bread-baking mission in a short period of time. It might not be the best bread in the world, and you probably couldn't compete with your neighborhood family-run bakery, but if you followed the recipe correctly, you'd have completed the assignment just fine.

Successful side hustlers create or obtain a similar recipe to take their hustle from idea to implementation. For each step of that process, there will be "ingredients"—the tasks you need to tackle, the resources you need to acquire, or the deliverables you need to produce—in order to complete your recipe for success. The more you can simplify your idea and break down the creation process into clear, specific steps, the easier it will be to get up and running quickly.

The specific recipe will be unique to everyone, so let's look at the process using Tanner's hustle as an example. After coming up with the idea and deciding on a format, his recipe for setting up this hustle required three steps: writing, website optimization, and revenue generation.

STEP 1: WRITING. Tanner got to work making a list of questions. Then, all he had to do was sit down and write according to those topics on his list. Those articles represented his first ingredients. He chose a crisp writing style that stayed on topic and encouraged readers to keep clicking to other articles. Once he had a good number of them answered thoroughly, he put them aside and moved to the next step.

STEP 2: OPTIMIZATION. As the classic Buddhist koan asks, if a website launches with no visitors, is it really there? Tanner knew that just as he'd need to write a lot of helpful articles, he'd also have to put effort into making sure those articles would be seen. That's where the next ingredient came in: he put his knowledge of websites and SEOs to work, setting up a simple site, choosing the right keywords, and monitoring search results to see which of his pages performed the best. Then he applied that method to all the other pages and continued to monitor performance each week.

STEP 3: REVENUE GENERATION. Tanner had a good idea, he knew how to write, and he knew how to get people to the website—but he wasn't done yet. He needed a revenue model! Fortunately, in this case there was an obvious one. The visitors he received were "targeted" (meaning they were there for a specific reason; everyone who came to the site was clearly interested in cruising), so it made perfect sense to install Google advertising, his final ingredient. The plan for getting paid was clear: bring people in, serve them well, and then get rewarded when they clicked ads. Everything that Tanner needed to do or source for this side hustle fit into one of those three steps. He went from idea to hustle in record time, and it paid off handsomely.

BREAD-BAKING BASICS

To understand how to create or gather the ingredients you need to launch, let's see how this resource-gathering process applies to two potential projects. In each scenario, we'll look at what you need to produce as well as a few additional components that relate to each project.

GOAL #1: CREATE A RÉSUMÉ SERVICE

SUMMARY: You want to help college students get more interviews and better job offers by helping them prepare résumés that will stand out in a sea of applications

INGREDIENTS: Website that presents the offer, accepts payment, and schedules appointments

STEPS:

1. **COPYWRITING:** Spell out your offer, including your promise, pitch, and price (refer back to Day 9 for a refresher on this).

2. **WEBSITE DESIGN:** In addition to posting all the information from step 1, build in a mechanism for getting paid, as well as a scheduling system where people can book appointments.

3. **MARKETING:** Come up with a plan for how you'll encourage happy students to refer you to their peers.

GOAL #2: DESIGN AND SELL CUSTOM-BRANDED JOURNALS

SUMMARY: You want to design and print a fun, unique journal that is different from everything else on the market

INGREDIENTS: The journals themselves, and a website that will show them off and accept payment from buyers

STEPS:

1. **DESIGNING:** Decide what type of journal you will produce, and what it will look like.

2. **PRODUCTION:** Figure out how and where the journals will be printed.

3. **MARKETING:** Brainstorm ways to get the word out about your journal to potential customers. Should you try a crowdfunding campaign to raise funds and generate early interest?

4. **SHIPPING:** Set up an efficient system for fulfilling orders and sending your journals to customers.

CREATE YOUR SHOPPING LIST

Just as no two recipes are exactly the same, the recipe for every side hustle is different. Your ingredients may vary from those in these three plans, but here are some common ones.

WEBSITE. Many, if not most, hustles these days should have some kind of website. A website is essentially an online home—and you probably don't want to be homeless. A website has several components: hosting, where the website lives; and a content management system, like Wordpress or Squarespace, that makes it easy to publish pages and posts. Don't overpay for a website: you can get all the bandwidth and space you need for as little as $5 a month.

SOCIAL MEDIA PROFILES. Don't worry about trying to be everywhere in the social media universe at once. Pick one or two networks and spend your time on those. However, *do* register your name (or your hustle's name, if appropriate) on the most popular networks—even if you don't intend to use them—to make sure no one else does first. Search "social name checker" to see several directories that will allow you to check for availability on many networks at the same time.

SCHEDULING TOOL. This is important for coaches, consultants, or anyone who makes time-based commitments that involve other people. Avoid the endless back and forth of "What time is good for you?" with a program that will display mutually acceptable times for each party.

WORKFLOW. A detailed sales or service process, or an on boarding campaign for your new customers. You'll learn how to make these on Day 15.

PAYMENT SYSTEM. This could include a shopping cart on your website, a PayPal account, an invoicing system, or any of the number of options you'll learn about in tomorrow's lesson.

Note: I haven't listed any specific software or brands here, because they may not be current by the time you read this. To get a list that is continuously updated, visit SideHustleSchool.com/resources.

TIME TO TEST THE RECIPE

A recipe is only as good as the finished product you take out of the oven. So as you craft yours, the answers to two questions should be at the front of your attention.

1. What will people experience after purchasing your offer?

2. What needs to happen for you to deliver that experience to them?

The first question will lead you to the finished product or service that you offer to your customers. The second will help you decide what recipe to choose and ensure that you have the ingredients you need to make it successful.

Tanner's primary ingredients were answers to cruise questions in the form of blog posts. Once he had the structure set up, all he had to do was write better and more useful posts, all the while optimizing his site to compete more effectively in search results.

In his case, the answers to the two questions above came naturally: people will receive comprehensive (yet easily accessible) information about what to expect on their vacation. Their lives will be improved because they can plan better and feel more confident prior to departure.

The great thing about Tanner's hustle was that once he mastered his process, it became much easier to repeat over and over again. Indeed, like with any good recipe, if you come up with a good process, your results should keep getting better and better each time you execute it.

And of course, Tanner would get paid—month after month. He'd charted his course and set sail on a sea of recurring income.

Set Up a Way to Get Paid

> You've got a lot more than just an idea now—
> you're well underway to a real-life side hustle.
> Before proceeding, make sure you've also got a
> real-life way to get paid real money for it.

Parker McDonald was fascinated by the world of side hustling. By day, he worked as an IT manager, but he wanted to earn extra money and begin building a long-term source of financial security. He'd heard about the website Fiverr, where he could post jobs he was willing to do for hire. He didn't have anything to lose, so he signed up and started bidding for small projects.

The initial results were hardly encouraging. He got some work—but it was for minimum wage pay. Fortunately, one of those initial projects soon led to something bigger. An overseas client looking for a native English speaker approached Parker to create a video for his small business. The video turned out well, and Parker was surprised at how much he enjoyed the work. The client referred him to other contacts, and within a few weeks he'd received several assignments for voiceover work, which paid more than the random proofreading gigs he first received through Fiverr. Plus, startup costs were extremely low: he simply purchased a $100 microphone and downloaded some free audio-editing software.

When he created his profile on Fiverr, the system asked for his bank account details. Twice a month, whatever money he'd earned during the previous payment period would automatically transfer to him. In less than a year and with very limited work hours, the voiceover hustle has brought in more than $8,000—more than enough to cover his car payment, a weekly date night with his wife, and the beginnings of a lifelong savings account.

IF YOU DON'T HAVE A WAY TO GET PAID, YOU DON'T HAVE A HUSTLE

It sounds obvious: if you want to make money, you need a way to get paid. Yet I continue to be surprised by how many retail websites have a checkout button that is difficult or impossible to find, or how many new consultants don't have a process in place to file invoices. I once had to follow up with a vendor five times to find out what I owed and how I could pay them—they made it hard work to give them money! Many side hustlers I've encountered have *some* way to get paid, but the process is far more difficult than it needs to be.[*]

Don't make this mistake. Before you launch your hustle to the world, you need a payment system in place, and the system you need will vary depending on what kind of hustle you're starting. Throughout this book, I distinguish between selling a product or providing a service, and on Day 12 you learned about the different pricing models best suited for both. With a product hustle, where you sell either a physical item or a digital one, your price should reflect the cost of expenses, plus the minimum acceptable profit

---

[*]   You may already know how you'll get paid for the hustle you're starting. If so, great! Feel free to skim the rest of this day's lesson and move to the next.

per item or per sale. With a service hustle, where you're essentially selling your time or expertise, you want to set your initial price according to your minimum acceptable hourly income, *or* charge a flat rate based on what your time is worth.

Just as your pricing model will often depend on which category your hustle falls into, so will the method of payment you choose to set up. If you're selling a product, a simple payment system will likely meet your needs; for a service hustle, you'll also need an easy method for invoicing customers.

SIMPLE PAYMENT SYSTEMS

If you already have a payment system set up, you may be able to skip this section. But if you're just starting out, or if you're looking to simplify, here are three good solutions. Each has advantages and disadvantages you should be aware of and factor into your decision.

PAYPAL. Tried and true and extremely simple, PayPal is used in nearly every country in the world and by more than 200 million customers. If you don't yet have a PayPal account, first pinch yourself to make sure you haven't been sleeping through the past twenty years. Then, head to PayPal.com and sign up for free. You can add a button or link to your website to accept funds through PayPal, or you can bill customers directly through the system.

SHOPIFY. If you sell products with a fixed quantity (as opposed to a service or a product with unlimited quantity, like an e-book or app), the benefits of this system are the easy-to-use shopping cart and inventory management tool. Additionally, you can create a basic website right from the interface. Hundreds of thousands of people use Shopify, and the service focuses on serving individual sellers instead of big businesses. To get a free trial and see if it works for you, visit Shopify.com/sidehustle.

STRIPE. This is a payment system that works with many other systems to take payments directly on your website. It's cheaper than PayPal and more customizable than Shopify, but it also requires more setup. Use this if you know what you're doing, or if your hustle is going well and you want to take things to the next level.

These are just a few of many payment systems out there, and depending on your level of tech savvy, some may be easier for you than others. Whichever you choose, make sure it's easy for you *and* your customers.

PAYMENT NOTIFICATIONS ARE FUN

Want to experience what it feels like to rob a cash register without going to jail? Connect your smartphone to your payment system, then turn on payment notifications. For best results, assign the payment notification an audio alert that sounds like a cash register ("cha-ching!").

Yes, I know—you're already getting bombarded with countless Facebook messages, texts, and probably a bunch of other stuff. Do you really want a stream of annoying notifications adding to that? Trust me: getting notifications that inform you of new money in your bank account will not be annoying. It will be *awesome*. If they do become distracting at some point, you can turn them off. Until then, experience the joy that arrives when your cash register phone announces a new sale.

SIMPLE INVOICES

Some hustles, generally service-based ones, require that customers or clients be billed at a certain point in the process. If it sounds like a lot of boring paperwork, think about it this way: without a means of promptly submitting invoices, then doing whatever follow-up is needed to make sure they are paid, you'll essentially be working for free.

Payment schedules can vary, but since we're keeping it simple, you probably want to choose one of these three:

- Payment in full prior to beginning work

- Partial payment prior to beginning work, the rest at completion

- Payment in full when the work is completed

Which of these you choose depends largely on what kind of service you're providing. If you think about it as a customer, you probably pay people and businesses in all three of these ways at different times. When you get on the bus to work in the morning, you don't pay "half now, half later." You hand the driver your money or ticket, and then they let you on the bus. If you're buying a cable or Internet subscription, however, you probably don't pay all at once. You pay a sign-up fee followed by a series of monthly payments, usually deducted automatically from your bank account. Last, when most of us go to the doctor or dentist, we usually give the receptionist a check or credit card (or sign the bill for insurance) on the way out the door.

Keep it simple and do whatever is common in your industry (though when you have a choice, getting payment in advance is almost always best). Whichever you choose, there's often more than one part to the task of setting up a payment option:

- Decide on the payment options you will accept (credit card, check, bank transfer, etc.)

- If invoicing, decide on how you'll prepare and submit invoices

- If invoicing, decide on a time frame and process for clients who don't pay promptly (for example: plan to send a follow-up email on the second day of their being late, then make a phone call if you still haven't been paid by the fifth day)

There's no need to invent an all new system of invoicing. Just make sure it's convenient for you, and seamless for your customers.

SIMPLE CONTRACTS

The goal of a contract is to cover your bases, while striking the right balance between your protection and good-faith efforts. Whether we realize it or not, all of us enter into contracts every day when we shop online or sometimes even buy something from a store.

You don't always need a detailed buyer's agreement for everything you sell, and in fact, an elaborate, highly restrictive contract can sometimes be off-putting. For example, I once hired someone to complete a small project for me. It wasn't very complicated and the total bill was around $250. She surprised me by sending over an eight-page contract that included all sorts of clauses and restrictions. I offered to pay in full even before she started, but I didn't sign that contract.

A very basic contract should specify what you'll do, how much you'll be paid, and when you'll get paid. That's it. As noted on Day 11, you can even complete it an email (yes, it's legally valid) by writing it out exactly like that:

1. What you'll do

2. How much you'll be paid

3. When you'll get paid

A basic contract should also specify any protections you require. For example, what if the work is only half complete? For creative work, is it clear who owns whatever is produced? Most of these terms can still be laid out in a couple of pages at most.

Setting up a way to get paid is pretty simple, but it's also critical. Money has to find its way to your bank account! Decide on at least one method of payment, and make sure it's ready to go (and working properly) before you launch.

Design Your First Workflow

You're well on your way and almost ready to send your hustle out into the world. By listing out your next steps in an ordered fashion, you'll prevent mishaps and feel more confident.

From the pastoral Quabbin Valley in central Massachusetts, Amanda MacArthur runs a content marketing agency with her husband. She's been doing this for six years and enjoys managing a team and serving software companies worldwide.

She also loves to cook, and she has a special diet known as ketogenic (like Paleo, but no starch or sugar). A few years ago she began posting recipes on a website, mostly so that she could keep up with them. Since her day job involves managing websites, she couldn't help but add a little marketing zest to the site, installing an email capture form and links to some affiliate products.

Without paying much attention, one day Amanda noticed that more than three thousand people had subscribed. *That's interesting*, she thought, but she was also busy at work and considered this a strictly personal hobby, rather than a potential side hustle. Finally, when the number of subscribers reached six thousand a few months later, she sent out the first email to the group. She said she was working on a cookbook—would any of them like to preorder?

To her surprise, a lot of them took her up on it. By the end of the day, she'd made $1,000.

For the next few weeks, she lived in fear that everyone would call her a fraud and ask for a refund. But instead, the emails she received were full of praise and thanks. Her recipe readers clearly liked what she had to offer.

As the website continued to grow in popularity, Amanda was approached by a publisher who wanted to create a print book featuring her recipes. Between that project and the original e-book, the hustle is now bringing in at least $2,000 a month. She feels like she *could* invest more time and see it take off even further, but she's also happy with the day job—so for now, she keeps the side hustle on the side.

CREATE A WORKFLOW AND PREPARE TO HUSTLE!

You've made your initial decisions; now it's time to put everything into motion. What happens next will transform you from someone who had an idea to someone who took action and turned their idea into reality. In the next section, we'll get much more specific about how your idea will be presented to potential customers. After that, we'll talk about how to send it out to those customers in a real-world test. To make sure you're ready, let's first create a list of everything that needs to happen along the way. This list is called a *workflow*.

A workflow is simply a series of activities or processes that must occur to complete a project. In the case of hustles, it's everything that needs to happen for customers to make a purchase *and* receive whatever they've paid for. Like all the other exercises in this book, you don't need fancy software or an engineering degree to create a workflow. You simply need to make some notes, either in list form or a more visual style, as you'll see in a moment.

In the story above, Amanda's customer workflow began long before she had actual customers: when she started posting recipes online free of charge and focused entirely on providing helpful information, rather than making a profit. However, she did one very smart thing that set her up for future sales: she added an invitation for readers to join an email list, thus opening the doors of communication in a way that didn't require them to visit the site all the time.*

The workflow for setting up that email list looked something like this:

EMAIL LIST SIGN-UP WORKFLOW

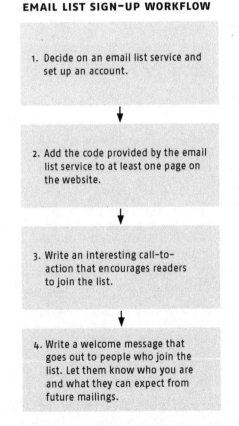

1. Decide on an email list service and set up an account.

2. Add the code provided by the email list service to at least one page on the website.

3. Write an interesting call-to-action that encourages readers to join the list.

4. Write a welcome message that goes out to people who join the list. Let them know who you are and what they can expect from future mailings.

---

*   Amanda's invitation was: "I'll send you my favorite keto-paleo recipes every week. 10 carbs or less!"

With this list, Amanda almost immediately transformed her blog visitors from mere readers into potential customers. When she decided to try selling that first e-book to all those people who looked to her for recipes, her workflow looked something like this:

CUSTOMER PURCHASE PROCESS WORKFLOW

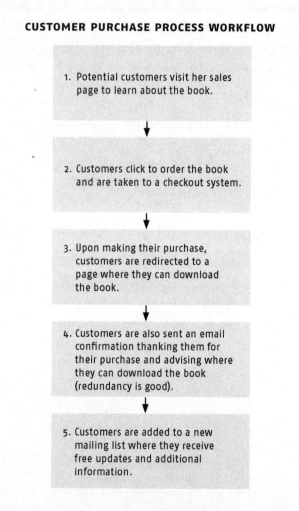

1. Potential customers visit her sales page to learn about the book.

2. Customers click to order the book and are taken to a checkout system.

3. Upon making their purchase, customers are redirected to a page where they can download the book.

4. Customers are also sent an email confirmation thanking them for their purchase and advising where they can download the book (redundancy is good).

5. Customers are added to a new mailing list where they receive free updates and additional information.

Notice that this workflow is described from the customer's perspective: someone who's interested in this kind of diet goes to her site, purchases the book, receives the book, and so on. Amanda's process for making all these things happen may be a bit different or require additional steps, but envisioning it from the perspective of her customers helped her ensure that she was capturing everything she needed to do to make her customers' experience as smooth as possible.

TROUBLESHOOTING

One of the best things about making a customer workflow is that it can help you pinpoint a few places where something could go wrong. For example, step 4 of Amanda's workflow requires that customers download their purchase after making payment. More than once I've set up a workflow like this, only to catch a mistake, like typing in the wrong download page URL or failing to upload the right files.

Fortunately, Amanda was smarter than me. She made sure to troubleshoot this process carefully, buying her own product using a different email address than the one she used to set up the account. She then made sure that everything worked as it should, first visiting the download page she was directed to after purchase, then checking her email to make sure the confirmation message came through, and finally downloading the book through both methods.

One way to troubleshoot any workflow is to test out the customer experience yourself, like Amanda did in the example above. Another is simply to ask: "What could go wrong?"

To break that down a bit, other troubleshooting questions might include:

- If your system relies on email communication, what if people don't get the email?

- If you're shipping out a product, what happens if people enter the wrong shipping address or an item goes missing?

- If you're scheduling a coaching session, does your calendar accommodate different time zones? What if one of you needs to change the appointment time?

By thinking through different problem scenarios, you may identify obvious solutions that will save time and hassle later. If people need to receive an email, for example, you can make that very clear when they purchase ("Important: Check your email right away for a message from us. If you don't see it within 24 hours, write to help@mysite.com").

You won't be able to prevent every mishap, of course. The best way you'll improve your hustle is through the real-world experience of interacting with customers. Still, the purpose of testing workflows is to prevent common, recurring errors that could derail your hustle.

WHAT ELSE NEEDS TO HAPPEN?

The examples in this day's lesson should get you thinking about your own workflow, but since every hustle is different, you still need to create your own master list. There are probably some specific processes associated with your idea that only you know about. Take some time to write them down in whatever format you prefer.

These questions may help:

- How will prospective customers or clients learn about your idea?

- What will happen after someone purchases or signs up for whatever you're offering?

- What else needs to happen in order for your customer to pay for and receive your service or product?

- How would you proceed if the book stopped here, but you still had to launch your hustle in the next twelve days?

Create your master list of tasks, actions, and next steps. The more detailed, the better. If you're not sure about something, that's okay—but list whatever tasks and ideas you can. You'll get more comfortable with workflows as you see how they can make life easier for both you and your customers.

Spend 10 Percent More Time on the Most Important Tasks

> Many new hustlers get caught up in trivial details that steal their time from important work. To avoid the trap of the mundane, keep your focus on just two things.

Oliver Asis works as a civil engineer for the State of California. He's also an amateur landscape photographer, with a good eye and a lot of technical skill. When a friend asked him to photograph her wedding, he was happy to say yes—but just an hour later, he started to panic as the reality of what he'd committed to set in. He'd never shot a wedding before, and he hadn't even been to a lot of weddings. He knew that most weddings follow a general protocol, and he knew to get plenty of photos of the bride, but he also figured that wedding photography was the kind of thing you don't really learn until you do it.

Plenty of people in Oliver's situation would have panicked and set out on a crash course to learn everything they could about wedding photography: enroll in a class at the local college, pore through a stack of instructional books, or maybe read everything to be found online about the subject. Oliver had a better idea. Instead of embarking on an all-consuming research project, he decided to invest his time in gaining actual experience by offering to shoot a wedding for a very low fee for the first couple who took him up on the offer. He posted the deal on Craigslist: *Cheap-but-hard-working wedding photographer available for hire; price is $250 to the first person who asks!*

He put it bluntly when he told me the story later: "I didn't want to mess up my friend's wedding, but if I messed something up for a stranger, I wouldn't feel as bad."

After he made an appointment to meet the frugal bride-to-be who took him up on the offer, he realized he didn't really have a portfolio to show her. Thinking quickly, he sifted through some of his favorite landscape photos—which didn't relate to weddings in any way, but were all he had—and sent a few off to the printer. Since the whole thing was an experiment, he figured that there was no point sinking hours and hours into taking a whole new set of photos. His time was better spent preparing for the upcoming job.

Fortunately, he didn't mess up the stranger's wedding. It was a learning experience that gave him more confidence for the next one, and the bride loved the photos. That first gig paid just $250 for a lot of work, and then his friend paid him $500 for hers the next month—but with more experience and a portfolio of actual wedding photos, he quickly became able to charge a lot more. He now does at least one wedding a month for a starting price of $3,500.

Oliver's story is a classic side hustler narrative. He didn't know how to do something, so he figured it out. The story also illustrates another important side hustle principle: do more of what's important, and less of what's not. Oliver didn't get caught up in lots of fussy details; he focused entirely on applying his skills to create a great customer experience.

Later, as he grew his hustle, he was also smart to focus on doing the things that would allow him to raise his prices to a much more reasonable amount. He chose to market to a higher-paying clientele and boosted the perceived value of his services by publishing the rave reviews he received. These two general areas, providing more value and making more money, should be your primary focus as you prepare to launch your hustle—and then as you grow it, too.

FOCUS AREA #1: CHANGE YOUR CUSTOMER'S LIFE

A lot of people are looking for a shortcut to success. In their mind, this shortcut is something that will allow them to "hack" their way to the front of the line or otherwise skip a lot of steps. With a side hustle, hacks are indeed helpful. They can allow you to be more efficient. They can help you be more productive. And to a certain degree, they can help you make more money.

But the best hack of all is to do something that makes a difference in people's lives, or at least the life of the ideal customer that you identified on Day 8.

The way you'll be successful in the long run has nothing to do with hacking. If your hustle is built on maneuvers or tactics, you don't really have an asset—you have a short-term opportunity that will end sooner or later. In Oliver's case, when he met with his first bridal client, he could have tried to impress her with a detailed explanation about all his technical equipment and gear. Or he could have gone into a long-winded monologue about his artistic philosophy and vison. Either conversation might have come natural to him as a photographer, but neither would matter much to the bride. Mostly, she wanted the answer to a simple question: Did he have everything he needed to do a good job?

He was already a good photographer. What he needed to learn was how to be a good *wedding photographer*. The single greatest thing he could do to prepare for his friend's wedding was to get experience at another wedding, so that's exactly what he concentrated on.

No matter what your hustle is, you should always focus on improving the experience for your customer. Methods for doing this could include:

- Underpromise, overdeliver. Manage expectations but go above and beyond whenever possible.

- Respond to unspoken needs. Sure, they hired you to complete a certain task—but is there something else they need that you could easily provide as well? If you uncover such a thing in the course of performing a service, offer to help with it at least once at no charge.

- Highlight positive results. If you report back to customers in some way, *show* them how your service has benefited them. They may not immediately realize how your actions make their life easier, more convenient, or more enjoyable (or all three), so gently point it out.

FOCUS AREA #2: MAKE MORE MONEY

The second area of focus relates to you. There are lots of great reasons to have a side hustle, but never forget that money is one of them. Your hustle must be profitable! As he gained experience, Oliver migrated away from gimmicks ("I'll shoot your wedding for $250") and made himself available to couples who had a larger budget. He could have kept on selling his service on Craigslist, but chances are he'd always be competing strictly on a cost basis, not a value basis. The selection of a wedding photographer relies heavily on reputation, so Oliver made sure his remained stellar.

Ways to make more money could include:

- Commit to a schedule of regular price increases.
  People understand that most businesses increase
  their price over time. Sometimes it's good to be the
  exception . . . but this isn't one of them.

- Pursue incremental revenue. Once you're making
  money, it's not usually that difficult to make more.
  Poke around to see what else you might be able to
  do that would earn additional income with little
  additional investment of time.

- Start a side hustle to your hustle! Most hustlers
  operate more than one hustle throughout their
  lives. Once you've built one project, ask yourself
  what's next. Guess what's better than two streams of
  income? It starts with the number three.

SPEND TWENTY-FIVE MINUTES A DAY DOING ONE THING TO GROW YOUR HUSTLE

Hustlers tend to fall in the trap of trying to do too much. And it's
not just busy hustlers; some of us small-business owners—those of
us who do this full-time—aren't any better. In fact, as a hustler you
have the built-in *advantage* of not being able to hustle all day long.
You need to work smart, not just hard.

Long ago, I lived on a hospital ship in West Africa. My day job
was as a volunteer aid worker. In the evenings and early mornings,
I moonlighted (literally) by working on a side hustle that was based
in the United States. It was just me and one assistant, both of us
working very limited hours—and as the hustle was taking off, there
was no shortage of things to do and emails to respond to. I sometimes felt overwhelmed trying to manage everything, especially
since my main priority was the work we were doing in post-conflict
countries like Liberia and Sierra Leone.

Somewhere around this time I got in the habit of accomplishing one task every morning that had nothing to do with *running* the business and everything to do with *growing* the business. My time was still limited—I usually had only about twenty-five minutes—but during that time I blocked out everything else and did only the task associated with growth. It helped that I carried a notebook around with me and wrote down ideas for my "Actually Make Something Time," as I called it. I made a rule to not open my laptop before beginning this session, without knowing what I wanted to do in those twenty-five minutes. Otherwise, I'd inevitably end up distracted and fail to accomplish anything significant.

Doing this first thing in the morning proved to have a number of advantages. For one, as the chaos of the day unfolded, I felt a sense of satisfaction that no matter what else happened, at least I'd accomplished that morning's "Make Something" task. I also noticed that if I missed the habit in the early morning, it was very hard to carry it over to the rest of the day. By the time I ended my day job, I was *tired*. I'd force myself to answer as many emails as possible, and I'd probably be able to complete a few other administrative tasks, but the odds of returning to that growth-oriented mindset at the end of the day were slim.

When you focus on what's important, you make a lot more progress. Don't let yourself get distracted from the two things that matter the most for your side hustle: the benefit for customers, and the income for you. Spend at least 10 percent more time on each of these areas, and spend less time on everything else.

Oliver's cheap Craigslist gig was great—it gave him good experience and he learned a lot through the process. But he didn't want to work for $5 an hour, the approximate take-home wage he earned after subtracting everything associated with preparing, shooting, and processing wedding photos for that first client. With that experience, and the one from his friend's wedding behind him, he felt far more confident in his ability to create a beautiful set of memories for future brides and grooms. Accordingly, he then raised his price to an amount that reflected the one thing that mattered the most: the joy he brought to the lives of his customers.

WEEK 3 RECAP!

You've gone from idea generation to offer creation . . . and now it's time to move to execution! Now that you have a solid offer to present your customers—along with a way to get paid for it—it's time to move on to the step you've been waiting for: *launch*.

— KEY POINTS —

- Ideas must turn into offers so that people can pay you for them. An offer includes a promise, a pitch, and a price.

- Use the cost-plus model to set your price. You want it to be low enough that you don't turn away or lose customers, but high enough that you can still earn enough money to make the hustle worth your time.

- Once your idea is more fully formed, create workflows and list every action your customer will need to go from discovery to purchase (then consider a few common scenarios to find solutions where something might go wrong).

- Make it as easy as possible for customers to pay you. Always start with simple technology. You can upgrade later if the hustle takes off.

- When you're not sure how to spend your hustle time, focus at least 10 percent more of your time on two things: change people's lives, and make more money.

WEEK 3: PREPARE FOR LIFTOFF

Day 11: Assemble the Nuts and Bolts ✓

Day 12: Decide How to Price Your Offer ✓

Day 13: Create a Side Hustle Shopping List ✓

Day 14: Set up a Way to Get Paid ✓

Day 15: Design Your First Workflow ✓

Day 16: Spend 10% More Time on the Most Important Tasks ✓

LAUNCH YOUR IDEA TO THE RIGHT PEOPLE

After careful planning, you're all set to take your offer into the world. The time is now!

WEEK 4: LAUNCH YOUR IDEA TO THE RIGHT PEOPLE

Day 17: Publish Your Offer!

Day 18: Sell Like a Girl Scout

Day 19: Ask Ten People for Help

Day 20: Test, Test, and Test Again

Day 21: Burn Down the Furniture Store

Day 22: Frame Your First Dollar

Publish Your Offer!

> When's the best time to get your offer out and
> see what happens? Usually before you're ready.

When the first version of the iPhone came out in 2008, Steven Peterson was excited. He'd been developing software for sixteen years and wanted to learn to build something on the brand-new Apple iOS platform.

At the time he was commuting from San Francisco to Palo Alto every day, a thirty-mile journey that can take up to two hours depending on traffic. Tens of thousands of people were commuting to and from the Bay Area every day, just like Steven, and every morning they all had the same question: What will traffic be like today?

A lot of public transit data was available online, but it wasn't easily accessible or understandable to most people. Steven had a hunch that the iPhone debut was more than just another product launch. He saw its potential to improve daily life, and it didn't hurt that millions of units had been preordered by eager consumers.

Apple planned to release the device with an online "App Store," where new buyers could load up their first smartphone with their choice of programs. Once the iPhone became a universal, must-have gadget, more than one thousand apps launched every day. But in the beginning, the platform was much more sparse and controlled, and it involved a rigorous approval process.

The week before the deadline to submit an app for consideration to be included on launch day, Steven was home sick from work. He decided to use his non-resting hours to hack together an app that would compile public transit and traffic data and present it in a visually pleasing, easy-to-understand style. He called it Routesy.

He was, by his own account, shocked when Apple emailed to notify him of the app's acceptance. The idea was great . . . the execution, not so much. It crashed a lot. The interface was ugly. A long list of planned features had been abandoned when he ran out of time.

He knew the project had a long way to go, but being included in the early launch provided motivation to keep working on it.

Monetization was a secondary goal for Steven. He made the app because he liked Apple and he liked making things. He also knew that a large group of people could benefit from a better solution to planning their morning commute, and that no one else had made something like Routesy. Still, the thought of earning extra cash was appealing, so he signed up for an advertising network that would display banner ads to users on the bottom of the screen.

On the day of the launch, the *San Francisco Chronicle* published a blurb about the app in the business section. Fittingly, Steven noticed it while he was standing in line waiting to get his first iPhone. It was exciting to see something he'd made go out to the world, or at least the world of early tech adopters who lived in the area. Given all the technical glitches, he didn't expect to make serious money from it, but when Apple published the very first revenue report the very first month the App Store was online, Steven's proceeds were approximately $2,700.

THE BEST TIME TO START WAS YESTERDAY

By now, you've heard me say it more than once: start your hustle before you feel completely ready. Why start sooner rather than later? Well, there are several reasons. The first is *proof of concept*, the validation that you're on to something. Even when you feel confident, you never know for sure if your idea is going to work until it comes to life. Therefore, the sooner you can begin to learn how customers respond to it, even if the data is incomplete, the better.

Steven had proof of concept; Apple's early acceptance of the app alone was evidence he was on to something. The iPhone launch momentum, combined with the early press he received, was additional proof that carried him through month one. Then, the $2,700 payout was more than sufficient to motivate him to keep improving the app.

The second reason to launch before you're ready is that perfectionists do not make for good hustlers. If you wait for perfection, your twenty-seven-day plan could morph into twenty-seven years. Ever talk to someone who's wanted to start a big project for a long time? Whether it's writing a book, creating a hustle, or any other number of endeavors, when you ask them how it's going, you often hear responses like these: "I'm thinking about it." ... "I'll start working on it soon." ... "I have more research to do first."

Those responses are also known as procrastination, a plague that infects most of us at some point or another. As soon as you identify something you want to do, yet feel hesitation or fear about parts of it, the desire to *take it slow* or just do other things kicks in. I speak from experience: as an author, my house is never cleaner than when I'm writing a book.

I also know, however, that if I can overcome this resistance, I'll be much happier when I actually get to work.

In doing the interviews for my daily Side Hustle School podcast,

I've heard stories upon stories of how people started before they were ready.

- A self-published romance novelist presells the next book in a series before writing it

- A mom creates a "Stressed Mommy" line of private label wine, without knowing anything about the wine industry

- Two friends start an "Uber for Lawncare" hustle with the goal of serving lawn care professionals, figuring it out as they go along (they end up making more than $1 million a year)

All these examples reinforce a guiding lesson of this whole book: "Done is better than perfect." Not sure exactly how to handle a coaching session? There's no better way to learn than by doing a coaching session. Don't know how much it will cost to ship your paintings to international buyers? Estimate it. If you then discover that your estimate is wildly off-base, just adjust your price for future orders. In short: when in doubt . . . start!

CREATE A FACEBOOK PAGE BEFORE MAKING A WEBSITE

Here's a simple thing you can do to kick yourself into gear right now: if you think you will *ever* use social media for your hustle, take ten minutes and create a Facebook page for it. You don't have to program, design, or do much of anything besides sign up and add a brief description of what you're selling. Why do this before making a website? Well, first, it's incredibly easy—might as well knock it off the list.

But that's not the only reason. As people begin to engage with your page, Facebook will automatically gather data about them.

Once enough visitors have arrived (typically around one thousand, though it may vary), you'll be able to access a section called "Insights," which includes a lot of detailed information that will help you better reach—and serve—those visitors as you refine your hustle.

You may also find the mere act of having a Facebook page (or a similar social media account) inspires you to move forward more quickly. Once you have something published, it feels real—and you'll want to complete whatever other steps you need to build it out further.

LAUNCH IN BETA

What if you aren't ready to launch? Well, you're hardly ever fully ready . . . so here's a trick. Go ahead and publish your offer, but add the label "beta" to it. You could also call it "early version" or any other phrase that sounds good. Doing so will allow you to continue working on it while also getting real feedback, and hopefully some sales as well.

You can remain in this "already launched but not quite ready" phase for as long as you'd like. Gmail was in beta for over five years while it had more than 300 million users. This became a bit of a joke in tech circles—how can a service with 300 million customers claim to be in development?—but the point is that there is no rule that says your beta phase, preview mode, or "coming soon" status has to end at a certain point. If it helps you feel better to clarify that everything isn't perfect yet, do so.

There's a special feeling you get when you put your project out into the world. Even if no one pays attention right away, you look at it and think *I made that*. You feel proud, and you should. Over time, as you achieve more side hustle goals and launch other projects, this special feeling can be its own kind of reward.

Steven released his public transport app before he felt ready, and by doing so he gained access to a passionate early adopter audience. From day one of the iPhone launch, eager Bay Area commuters began downloading and using the app. Nearly a decade later, it has almost forty thousand users every weekday and has been downloaded by nearly half a million people. It also produces a steady income of at least $7,500 a month, allowing Steven tremendous flexibility to design the rest of his life however he sees fit.

Your time is now, hustler. There's more to be done, but we're moving past the planning phase. Everything else can happen while your hustle is live. We're moving into the world of action.

Sell Like a Girl Scout

> Even with a great product or service, and a
> great offer to make your pitch, magic money
> doesn't usually fall from the sky. Channel your
> inner Girl Scout and make some sales!

Before beginning a consulting career and pursuing a side hustle, Julie Wilder owned an organic restaurant for more than a decade. That business was rewarding, but as you can imagine, it was also a ton of work. Julie was also passionate about astrology. In her limited free time, she designed an astrology calendar and updated it every year. Several times she had thought about doing something more with it, but with so many hours taken up by the restaurant, she continued to defer the idea.

Astrology is a huge, global market. It's also a bit controversial, which is a good sign for a side hustle—it shows that people are passionate and have strong opinions about it. You don't want to go into an industry or niche where no one feels strongly one way or another. Despite the size of the market, until very recently there were only three main competing products for sale—and they all had very similar, new-agey art styles. That's fine for those who like that aesthetic, but there are many other people who might be interested in astrology but would prefer a more contemporary design. Julie had identified an underserved niche in the market, and in fact she uses the word *disruptive* to describe her hustle—by creating a modern, unisex design that is visually pleasing, she's been able to reach an audience of people who had never been interested in buying an astrology calendar before.

Finally, after updating the design for several years, she decided to try selling the calendar on etsy.com, the online marketplace for handcrafted items. It was mostly an exercise in curiosity, but right away, people seemed to like what she had to offer. It helped that there wasn't anything quite like it on the market—so after she sold the restaurant, she decided to spend some time exploring the hustle before starting an all-new, different career. Within a few months she had made $5,000 with minimal effort and virtually no investment. Aside from a few minor expenses for initial materials, the hustle supported itself from its very first week.

With manufacturing costs of $1 per calendar and a product that sells for $15, these profit margins are much better than any she could have made running the restaurant—and the work is far less stressful.

Julie had clearly identified a need, or at least a big gap in the marketplace that she thought people would respond to. And respond they did, with more than $5,000 in orders based solely on the free listings that etsy offered sellers. Julie didn't stop there, though. If people responded so well with no marketing at all, what would happen if she put in some effort?

The next step was to work a bit more on that marketing plan. She made several video tutorials and wrote a number of blog posts. To reach out beyond her existing circle of friends and acquaintances, she joined Facebook forums on astrology, where she then shared her videos and blog posts. Next, she contacted six influential astrologers and sent them a free calendar. It was one part thank-you for wisdom they'd shared throughout the year, and one part clever sales tactic, as she hoped that they'd share the calendar with their followers.

A TALE OF TWO HUSTLES

Where I live in Portland, Oregon, it's impossible to walk down a major downtown street without being interrupted by at least one person asking for donations on behalf of various causes. Being accustomed to constant rejection, these canvassers have learned to come up with creative pitches to get the attention of passersby. "Do you have a minute for the polar bears?" they might ask. "Do you care about the state of the endangered wood rat?"

Framed like that, it's hard to say no.

Yet even though these methods can be effective, they're highly annoying. The organizations that put the canvassers on the street see it as a numbers game: ninety-nine people might ignore them, but if one person gives in and makes a decision, that person could become a lifelong supporter—thus justifying the cost of paying the canvassers and continuing to keep them out on the streets.

Contrast this fund-raising tactic to another one that also takes place outside grocery stores, in parking lots, and elsewhere a few weeks every year. When springtime comes around, the flowers blossom, the birds rejoice, and best of all—Girl Scout cookies go on sale. If you're not familiar with Girl Scout cookies, you've had a hard life and should correct this imbalance as soon as possible.

The point is, each spring, Girl Scouts (known as Girl Guides in some countries) suit up in their official garb, set up shop outside grocery stores and shopping centers, and hustle. Their pitch is as basic as could be: "Would you like to buy some Girl Scout cookies?" There's no throwing themselves in your path down the sidewalk, no questioning your compassion for the struggles of baby polar bears, and little salesmanship—and shoppers buy boxes by the dozen.

One of the two pitches you just read about is manipulative and designed to throw you off. The other is compelling and creates no sense of guilt whatsoever, at least aside from what you'll feel after you eat an entire box of cookies in a day. Which kind of salesperson would you rather be, the street solicitor or the Girl Scout?

BE THE GIRL SCOUT, NOT THE STREET SOLICITOR

Your hustle is out, and you're now open for business! Chances are, however, you won't see a flood of activity as soon as you click the publish button, send the email, or post that social update. So what then?

Remember, neither customers nor money falls from the sky. You need a strategy to actually *sell* your offer. And you want that strategy to have a lot more in common with that of the Girl Scouts, who still have to hustle but do so in a perfectly natural, non-aggressive way.

Granted, delicious cookies sold by children are one of the easiest things to sell—and that's exactly the point: Girl Scout cookies sell not because of a manipulative pitch, or because of pushy sales tactics. They sell *because people like them.*

Even if you're not eligible for Girl Scout membership, you can still adopt their methods for your hustle. And if you're resistant to sales or marketing in general, remember two things:

1. You've put in a lot of work on your hustle. You're proud and excited of what you've made. You owe it to yourself to take the next steps to set yourself up for success.

2. The people who need your hustle *want* to be marketed to! They are waiting to hear about it. If you don't make it through the noise and reach them, they'll never have the chance to check out what you've made.

Let these principles guide your next steps. Whether you're in it for the long term or just want to make some quick sales, you need a strategy to consistently market your offer!

WHEN IN DOUBT, SEND THE EMAIL

I once had a large group of people on an email list I hadn't written to in a long time. I wanted to promote something new I'd made, but I worried about flooding inboxes. My fear was that my subscribers would be annoyed by the communication—that I was reaching out after all that time simply because I had something to sell.

I decided to take the risk and included a note at the top saying "Hey, I'm back!" Indeed, I received a small number of annoyed replies. But to my surprise, I received far more notes from readers saying that they'd missed me. One even emailed me to say "Can you subscribe me to every list you have?"

These replies made me realize that I'd actually been too conservative in my marketing. After that experience, I started emailing more frequently. Remember as well that if some people unsubscribe to a mailing list (or otherwise communicate their lack of interest), that's not always a bad thing. They may not have been the ideal customer for your offer anyway, and once they're gone, it will be easier to focus on the people who are.

LEAD WITH BENEFITS, BACK THEM UP WITH FEATURES

Even if you have the best product or service in the world, that won't do you much good if nobody knows about it. Girl Scouts don't sell $700 million worth of cookies a year (approximately 200 million boxes!) just because they're delicious, but rather because *everyone knows* they're delicious.

So as you begin working to spread the word about your offer, you want to make sure that in all your communication, you're letting people know just how great your product or service is. This means you'll lead with benefits: How will it help people? How will it make their lives easier, better, more fun, or more fulfilling? Remember to keep the benefits clear, specific, and immediately obvious.

At the end of this course, users will_____

_____.

By buying this widget, customers will _____

_____.

I will improve my clients' lives by _____

_____.

The best benefits tend to relate to an emotional need of some kind. For example, people want to take dance lessons to lose weight and feel more attractive. They want someone to look after their dog so they don't feel guilty about leaving him at home while they're at work. They want an astrology calendar because they like the idea that the position of the moon and stars can affect their lives.

Benefits should help people *feel better*. You don't always want to mention these emotional needs explicitly, but you should keep them in mind as you craft your language. The dog sitter might not come right out and say "Leave your dog with me and feel less guilty for abandoning him all day"—but they very well might say, "With my pet-sitting service, your dog will be loved, walked, played with, and cared for while you're away from home." See how it works?

Then, it helps to back up your benefit with features. Does your pet-sitting service include two thirty-minute walks a day, and up to three daily email updates? Does your guide to ballet include ninety-nine dance steps? That's great—make sure people know about it. Julie made sure her potential customers knew that her calendar featured a fresh, modern design and didn't assume that people who used it were already experts about astrology.

Even the best salespeople sometimes get benefits and features mixed up. Here's a good rule of thumb: benefits are the ways in which a product will improve someone's life; features are the details that demonstrate how. Both are important, but if a customer doesn't believe that your offer will make their lives better, a long list of features won't help. Always lead with benefits!

Remember when you wrote a letter to your ideal customer? You may want to start writing the sales copy for your offer based on what you said when you finished the statement: "My ideal customer struggles with . . ."

Let's say your ideal customer struggles with time management. Your sales copy might say "You'll save forty minutes a day with this tool that triages your email, showing you what's important and deferring everything else until after your lunch break." Here, saving forty minutes a day is the benefit, and the ability to triage and filter your email is the feature. Mentioning both is key to making your sales pitch compelling and persuasive.

Finally, when presenting your offer, establish value before introducing price. Ever visited a new gym you're thinking of joining? When you ask "How much does it cost?" you'll rarely get a straight answer right away. First, you'll get a friendly sales rep who offers to show you around. Only at the end of the process, after you've been impressed with all the fancy equipment and spin classes, will they sit down with you at a desk to discuss pricing. As you present your offer, remember to tell stories (and show photos or other media if you can) about how valuable, helpful, or awesome it is. Lead with value!

"YOU DON'T WANT A DRILL, YOU WANT A HOLE."

I once received an email from a reader who was seeking advice. Here's what she wrote: "I've started a résumé writing and LinkedIn profile writing business which is really starting to take off, but I can't figure out how to sell more to my existing customers with this business. Any ideas?"*

I responded by suggesting that she consider *why* people want help with their résumé and profile. Is it because there is intrinsic value in those things by themselves? (Spoiler: not really.) More likely, they want to improve their résumé or profile because they believe it will increase their chances of getting a job, or getting a better job. Or they think it will help them connect to more of the right people, or ultimately be more successful in a variety of ways. Put another way, people don't buy a drill because they want a drill; they buy a drill because they want a hole. The drill is just the means to that end.

By thinking about it like that, I told her, I bet there are a lot of different opportunities to help these people further—and if they already trust you, having had a good experience with the first thing they purchased, they are very likely to buy something else.

Always think about what people *really* want and why they want it. With that information in hand, it's much easier to figure out how to offer them the tools that will help them get it.

HOW TO SELL MORE GIRL SCOUT COOKIES

A few years back, eight-year-old Markita Andrews won a national contest to sell more cookies than any other Girl Scout in America.

---

* As I was writing this chapter, I received a LinkedIn request from someone who claimed to be a "mangement consultent." Always proofread your online profiles!

The grand prize was a trip around the world, which just so happened to be her eight-year-old self's lifelong dream.

How did she do it? In an appearance on *The Tonight Show*, she gave this answer:

"I just went to everyone's house and said, 'Can I have a $30,000 donation for the Girl Scouts?'

"When they said 'No,' I said, 'Would you at least buy a box of Girl Scout cookies?'"

She ended up selling more than $80,000 worth of cookies.

The lesson: If you want to sell more Girl Scout cookies—or anything else—don't be pushy, but also don't be afraid to get creative, and don't be afraid to make the ask.

Julie's calendar was successful in part because it was different, but it was a lot *more* successful because of the effort she put into being proactive about going after her ideal customers. She wasn't shy about reaching out to influencers in her industry and encouraging them to spread the word. By making videos and posting to Facebook forums, she got her calendar in front of people who genuinely wanted what she had to offer. From then on, it was easy—a great product meets an ideal customer, and a sale is made.

Chances are, even with a great product, your hustle won't sell itself. Don't be afraid to take a page from the Girl Scouts: set up a table on the proverbial sidewalk and invite people to buy.

Ask Ten People for Help

No man is an island, and few side hustles thrive without the help of friends and supporters. As you begin hustling, don't hesitate to ask everyone you know to join the cause and get the word out.

Until recently, Brianna Faith's "day job" involved being a high school student. As many of us can recall, the high school experience, or simply being a teenager in general, can be an emotional roller coaster. Even if you have a good home and don't lack for anything, you're still going through a lot of changes and preparing for adulthood.

Unlike most teenage girls, Brianna had never worn a lot of makeup, partly because she felt shy and uncomfortable attracting attention to herself. When she was sixteen, however, she made a change. She started wearing red lipstick, then gained the confidence to slowly work her way up to other colors. Eventually she graduated to neon blue, and from there she realized that no one really cared what color makeup she was wearing—and she felt as though she could finally be herself.

Brianna had been interested in entrepreneurship since an even younger age. The self-confidence she found in wearing bright lipstick colors inspired a new mission: to help other people feel more confident and not afraid to express themselves through bold cosmetics.

Her initial idea was to create a wholesale business, but then a mentor who had a bit more experience showed her how the world of consignment—where products are delivered essentially made-to-order, with commissions paid to their creators—worked. That's when she realized she wouldn't have to wait until she was older and had been to college to launch a side hustle. She could begin experimenting with cosmetic sales almost immediately.

As the holiday season rolled around, Brianna started asking for favors. By way of another mentor she had met through the first, she was able to get a small, unoccupied retail space in downtown Victoria, British Columbia, where she could operate a pop-up store for a whole month at no charge. Since she was selling on consignment and the space was free, her costs were extremely low. She spent only about $200 on a small amount of decor, some stationery, and signage.

The shop was up and running within ten days of Brianna's first learning about the space, and she kept it open for the next month. Thanks to lots of shopping during the holidays, by the end of the month she had cleared a profit of more than $7,000, $2,000 of which she donated to charity. Brianna is now planning to develop her own product line for her next adventure in retailing—and she's not waiting to finish college before she makes it happen.

WITH A LITTLE HELP FROM YOUR FRIENDS

Make no mistake, Brianna worked hard. For the whole month of her holiday break, the store was open every day except one, and she was there on-site from 7:30 in the morning until 8:00 at night.

When she got home, she answered emails and prepared for another long day. This kind of pace might not be sustainable in the long term, but that's okay. For a seasonal store that was a major opportunity for this young entrepreneur, she was more than willing to give it her all.

Still, even with her tireless work ethic, the store wouldn't have been a success through her efforts alone. At each stage of the process, she relied on outside help.

For example, when I asked her how she got people to show up, her answer was simple: she was excited about her project, and her enthusiasm was contagious. But that's not all. When her first mentor connected her with other leaders from a local business incubator, those leaders were impressed with Brianna's initiative and ambition. They helped her quickly learn how to run a point-of-sale (POS) system, do the bookkeeping, and manage her inventory. To run the shop, she started out by putting her friends to work. Soon, even without her having to ask for it, other help began to show up. An elderly man donated some gold-plated mugs that she was welcome to sell at whatever price she could get. Another man brought cakes from the coffee shop upstairs every day for a month.

In short, Brianna can attribute her success to her youthful ambition and work ethic, combined with the help of a small army of supporters who helped bring her vision to light.

DON'T BE AN ARMY OF ONE

Even though a side hustle can be a solo undertaking, you're not alone out there, or at least you shouldn't be. As you launch your new hustle, you'll want to reach out to a few key people for help—just like Brianna did. What kind of help? Ideally, you want a mix of people who can help with a variety of areas and perform a few different kinds of favors. Some people may have more than one role, but you can generally group them in one of four categories:

SUPPORTERS: general cheerleaders who can provide support and pitch in in various ways

MENTORS: guides or experts who give you specific feedback and advice*

INFLUENCERS: trusted authority figures who have the ability to connect you with potential customers and help you get the word out

IDEAL CUSTOMERS: people who represent your avatar and can offer detailed, honest opinions on the many "Should I do this or that?" questions you'll have

Your path will be easier if you identify and recruit these people early in the process. Some may come along later, as happened for Brianna, but starting with a few of them in your corner will give you a leg up.

DON'T "SPRAY AND PRAY." INSTEAD, BE SPECIFIC

As important as it is to ask people for help, you also don't want to ask *too many* people. Asking everyone you know for a favor is a lot like trying to serve everyone in the world with your hustle. Just as you'll be much more successful when focusing on a specific customer group, you'll also likely see far better results from asking specific people to help you reach those customers.

"Spray and pray" marketing may work in some rare cases, but even when it does, the success won't last long. Most of the time, merely blasting out a message is ineffective. That's why you should

---

* Choose mentors carefully, and don't buy into the common belief that everyone needs one. If you already know what you want to do, you just need to figure out how to make it happen.

start with a specific list of ten people to help you spread the word—more than a few, but less than everyone you know.

Think long and hard about your ten people. Make your list, and then write or call each person to tell them about your project. Remember that everyone is busy (including you!), so get to the point quickly, and be sure to include a specific "ask" so that people can easily say yes or no.*

I get a lot of pitches from people requesting my help or advice on something and naturally I'm not able to respond to all of them. Over the years I've seen good pitches, terrible ones, and a large majority that don't really stand out either way. Based on this experience, here's some subjective advice for asking for favors in a way that will get you the answer you want.

- Ask for one specific thing, not a shopping list.
  Make sure that one thing is something the person
  is actually able and well positioned to do. If you
  need help marketing your project on social media,
  for example, don't ask the friend who doesn't use
  Facebook or Instagram.

- Explain one thing about yourself and something
  about why and how your hustle will help people.

- Don't overdo the flattery. Feel free to say something
  nice about the person when explaining why you've
  come to them for help, but no need to go on and on.

---

* In my last book, *Born for This*, I shared the story of the 100-Person Project, an exercise created by a brand consultant who wanted to improve her business targeting. She scheduled a series of fifteen-minute phone calls (yes, with one hundred people!) and had completely transformed the business by the time she concluded the project. That book includes the complete exercise that you can replicate in your own way.

- Gently follow up if you don't hear back—but only once, and not right away. Give people at least a few days to respond.

- Don't expect everyone to say yes, and be gracious no matter the response.

On that last point: please do not make the other person feel guilty if they can't help right now. In fact, don't respond in any sort of negative way. Write back and say "Thanks so much for considering, I really appreciate it." Maybe that person will help later. Maybe you'll make a connection and they'll remember you when something else comes along. If nothing else, at least you won't sabotage the relationship.

DON'T BE "THAT GUY"

The golden rule of relationship building is: do not be "that guy." Who is "that guy"? A few examples from my inbox:

- The LinkedIn contact who asked for personal introductions to a dozen well-known people—despite the fact that I didn't even know the person who was making the request!
- The marketer who emailed to ask me to promote an offer, then when I politely declined because the offer wasn't a good fit, responded, "That's okay, you were on my list but I didn't really want your help." (Gee, thanks.)
- The hyper-persistent person who sent the same request to me via email, voice mail, and *three* social networks—all in the same hour—because they "just wanted to make sure I saw it." Believe me, I saw it!

Remember, it's a small world. People talk, and if you do cringeworthy things like the ones on this list of true stories, the word will get around. Be the person everyone wants to help, not "that guy" they try desperately to avoid.

A year later, Brianna had finished high school and began college. Encouraged by her early entrepreneurial success, she also had her eye on other goals. Could she have succeeded in her cosmetics hustle on her own? Maybe—she was certainly hardworking and determined. But fortunately, she didn't *have* to go it alone. By recruiting her friends, new mentors, and even the guy at the mall who brought cakes, her holiday pop-up shop was destined to succeed.

Remember, no man is an island. As you build your hustle, don't hesitate to ask for a little help from your friends.

Test, Test, and Test Again

> When you're beginning a new hustle, you
> don't usually know which approach will be
> the most effective. To find out, try different
> things and keep a record of results.

In Rockton, Pennsylvania, serial hustler Gabby Orcutt works as a commercial sales rep in the natural gas industry. She's also a certified yoga teacher, a photographer, and a lifestyle course facilitator. Oh, and on top of all that, she has young kids at home. How she does all these things, I'm not sure, but in case they weren't enough to keep her busy, a few years ago she started an all-new hustle—completely by accident.

Social networks come and go all the time, but a few of them end up leaving a mark on popular culture. Pinterest is one of those networks that has had a huge influence on the online world, reaching over 175 million users at its peak. The site revolves around the sharing of images and short posts known as pins. It has a very high female demographic—women are the most frequent users—and some people take it very seriously, spending hours a day on the site even with no commercial interest or desire to generate income at all. They just like pinning!

Still, whenever a large number of people is spending a large amount of time on a shared experience, there are usually a number of ways to make money from it. Like a lot of Pinterest users, Gabby started using the site just for fun, but her entrepreneurial mindset quickly led her to think, *Hey, I wonder if this could lead to something more.*

A lot of side hustles come from paying attention to how groups of people like to spend their time online. Gabby's was one of them: she found a company that manages campaigns for brands looking to get more exposure to particular audiences. She signed up and began directing some of her pins to their campaigns—but only when she felt it was a good and natural fit for her audience.

In the eyes of brands, Gabby is known as an influencer, which basically means that she has a lot of followers. There aren't a lot of other qualifications, since a network of followers speaks for itself. Because of all those loyal followers, she was able to monetize her passion project by getting companies to pay for website traffic that she sends them through the pins she posts.

In the first month, she earned more than $1,000. She couldn't believe she had just been paid to look at photos on the Internet and post her favorites, but the money was real.

This was a side *side* hustle from her many other projects, and initially she hadn't spent a lot of time on it. After that first month, though, she got pretty serious and decided to become a lot more active. Every day for weeks, in that very limited free time she had, she pinned and pinned and pinned—first thing in the morning and last thing at night. When she couldn't sleep, she woke up and pinned some more.

In addition to working hard, Gabby also worked smart. Pinterest is organized by boards of related images. Gabby has a lot of boards related to crafts and photography, which are very popular Pinterest categories, but she also has her boards broken down into smaller categories. By experimenting with different options over time, she's learned how to tailor her pins to those specific interests.

Especially in their early days, social networks tend to have a phenomenon of "the rich getting richer" where someone who has a lot of followers is likely to gain a lot more, more so than someone who's new—so after a while, momentum kicked in. She noticed that it also helps to follow other influencers who have a large following, so she did that, sometimes piggybacking on their followers by repinning their content and commenting on their popular pins. As a result, Gabby's network grew and grew, from tens of thousands to hundreds of thousands and finally to more than one million, Best of all, Gabby's Pinterest endeavor has made over $40,000 over the course of three and a half years. She wasn't a celebrity, even an online one. She was just smart in figuring out how to give people something they want.

THE DATA DOESN'T LIE

If your first hustle is a success, you may think you're a marketing genius. And maybe you are! But maybe you just got lucky. Or most likely, you're smart *and* you got a little lucky. The point is, you can't necessarily identify every variable that might lead to success or failure in any particular hustle. To find out if you're right about something, you have to test it.

Testing has a reputation of being dry and boring. But it's only boring in the way that making lots of money is boring. There's an old saying: the data doesn't lie. When you look at the data, you're not relying on intuition; you're relying on reality.

HOW TO DO A SIMPLE A/B TEST

One of the simplest experiments you can do is called an A/B test. This is just like a blind taste test, where you try two different soft drinks (or coffees, or anything) and choose which you prefer without knowing the brands or names. To A/B test your hustle, you might present customers with two versions of your product or offer and see which one people tend to select. Or, to do A/B testing on your website, you might create two versions of a page and direct half your traffic to one and half to another. Over time, you can easily see which version performs better—then you switch to that version and test something else.

Remember back on Day 5 when you did your back-of-napkin projections? The variables you identified there are the perfect things to test. Consider the example of the bird-watching class, where you weren't sure whether to charge $49 or $79. Well, set up two versions of the registration page, one for $49 and one for $79, and randomly direct half of your visitors to each. Then you look at the *conversion rate* (how many people sign up divided by the total number of people who saw the offer) for each. You may find that charging $79 instead of $49 doesn't affect bird-watchers' purchasing decisions much. If so, great! Now you know you can go ahead and charge the higher price, without worrying about losing customers.

DON'T TEST THE COLOR OF YOUR ORDER BUTTONS

A lot of people get sidetracked by testing tiny stuff. They've heard about how Amazon.com famously tests everything from how prices are displayed to the color of order buttons. The thing is, Amazon has 250,000 employees, sells approximately 480 million different items, and deposits at least a bigillion quadrillion dollars into its bank accounts *every day.*

Amazon's sales volume is so huge that if the company can manage to improve its conversion rate by just the tiniest sliver of a per-

---

* Precise estimates are hard to come by. Studies show it's at least a gillion quadrillion. Or maybe just a lot of money.

centage, it could mean hundreds of thousands of dollars of extra revenue. But you are not Amazon. You don't need to test everything. You just need to test *the things that matter most.* Start with the big stuff! Here are the big three:

1. Your product or service (what you offer)

2. Your offer (how you present it)

3. Your price (how much it costs)

You should avoid running more than one A/B test at a time, because then you can't know which factor influenced the different results. However, you should continue running *different* A/B tests, one after another.

For example, say you run a test comparing a 10 percent discount with a promotion for free shipping. You discover that free shipping is more appealing to your customers, so that becomes part of the new offer. What do you test next? Maybe you try putting free shipping up against a bulk purchase discount, or maybe you combine free shipping with the original 10 percent off to see if customers respond any differently to that versus the free shipping at the regular price.

Over time, you'll gain more and more information about what your ideal customer wants, and what they are willing to pay.

NEXT STEPS

All that should keep you busy as we approach our final week. But as important as testing is, remember to not miss the forest for the trees. You'll probably see far greater results from testing these three major variables than from the small things. Still, if you do decide to take a deeper dive into the world of testing, there are plenty of other variables to compare. Here are just a few to consider:

- Long vs short copy on your sales page

- Word order, especially in headlines and calls to action

- Website navigation and user experience

- Free trial vs low-priced trial (or vs no trial)

- Testimonials from happy customers vs experts' ratings or reviews *

- Hard sell vs soft sell (or both)

Just remember that all this testing can turn into a side hustle rabbit hole, so don't jump down it until you're sure that your offer itself is solid.

BE CAREFUL OF FALSE POSITIVES

A friend told me a story of some A/B testing he was doing for a larger brand. He had what he thought was a great idea: to change the call to action on the order page for a software subscription business. His change resulted in a *major* increase in click-throughs—more than 40 percent! Before he congratulated himself and booked a trip to Vegas, though, he watched the data for a few more days.

Alas, something was wrong. More people were clicking through, but far fewer were converting to actual sales. Meanwhile, the control page (the one that doesn't change) maintained the same level of sales, which made more money for the company in the end. Why? Who knows. But the data doesn't lie, so that's why you test. He abandoned the new call to action and went back to the original.

---

* These are two different forms of "social proof," an important factor in many purchasing decisions.

Pinterest was ideal for this kind of immediate testing. Gabby could upload a pin and know within an hour if it was a hit or not. As time went by, she got better at predicting which pins would go over the best with her rapidly growing audience. She also branched out a little, adding new "boards" that featured different, but related topics. By working hard *and* smart, she grew her following to more than one million people. Almost every month, she received a new contract for brand advertising that brought in at least $1,000.

As we've seen with other hustles, pinning for dollars may not last forever—but Gabby isn't complaining. She'll keep cashing those checks for as long as they continue to arrive.

Burn Down the Furniture Store

> Deals, discounts, and special offers are your not-
> so-secret weapon to encourage customers to
> purchase. There's a very good reason that so many
> stores "go out of business" every three months.

Long before he started a side hustle selling handcrafted stone and slate on etsy, the online crafts marketplace, Andrew Church of Waterford, Pennsylvania, had always been curious and ambitious. A former champion wrestler in college, he held down a part-time gig as a referee while working as an industrial engineer for GE.

That curiosity, in addition to a love of woodworking, led him to experiment with an unusual project. He took a slab of slate and cut it into the shape of his last name written in script letters. He planned to put the sign on the roof of his house and have that be the end of it. Once he bought the saws to cut the slate, however, he realized what a unique material it was. It was versatile, not that difficult to manipulate, *and* there weren't a lot of other people using it so creatively.

In a burst of inspiration (and a bit of state pride), he decided to make a bunch of Pennsylvania-shaped cutting boards out of locally reclaimed slate. That's how he ended up listing his creations on etsy, which seemed like a natural place for such things. And that's why he soon received a very nice email notifying him that a stranger had bought something from his brand-new online shop.

After that first notification, another one arrived a few days later, and before too long he was seeing orders on a regular basis. He didn't have a grand strategy for his hustle, but a holiday was coming up. On a whim, he decided to reach out to his Facebook followers and brand-new email list with an offer: for that one day only, they'd get 20 percent off their purchases.

Announcing that sale was like turning on a faucet. In less than a day, he sold more than he had in the past two weeks combined. Several new customers wrote to say they'd been looking at his cutting boards for a while, but just hadn't been able to commit to making the purchase. When the limited-time offer came around, that was just the incentive they needed to reach for their wallets.

DEALS, SALES, AND SPECIAL OFFERS: YOUR NOT-SO-SECRET WEAPON

If you've ever seen a "going out of business" sale at a furniture store that then opens up again a short time later, you're not the only one. With so many fire sales, you'd think the store owners are purposely burning down the store. These stores have such sales because they know they work, even if the tactic of closing and reopening again is hardly subtle.

The right kind of sale or special offer is like pulling up to a battlefield in a tank. Everyone knows what a tank is, and everyone can see the tank coming from a mile away. But do people sit up and pay attention? Well, yeah—it's a tank!

Have you ever responded to an offer for *something you didn't even want*, just because it was on sale? Of course you have—everyone has. Human beings are conditioned to respond to deals. Everyone loves getting something for less.

Offering some kind of sale or special offer is perhaps the most effective not-so-secret weapon you have in your side hustle arsenal. This doesn't mean you need to slash your prices or give away the store for free.* There's more than one way to use special offers to get people excited about your offer, but most of them involve creating the sense that (a) this is special, and (b) it won't be around forever.

Here's a brief list of *some* of the types you've probably seen:

- **DISCOUNT:** a percentage or dollar amount off the regular price

- **"FLASH" OR FIRE SALE:** a temporary, widespread price reduction

- **REBATE:** a discount provided *after* purchase

- **BUY ONE, GET ONE FREE (OR SIMILAR):** an incentive to receive something else after making a purchase

- **REFER-A-FRIEND:** a reward provided for bringing in new customers

- **FREQUENT SHOPPER PROGRAM:** a reward provided for spending more or spending more often

- **FREE SAMPLES OR TRIAL OFFERS:** designed to demonstrate a product or service before purchase

- **RANDOMIZED DISCOUNT:** a variable percentage or dollar amount off the regular price

- **CONTESTS:** a competition or randomly awarded prize

---

*   Life lesson: if you're going to sell your soul, be sure you get a good price.

The most important thing about these offers is that they are valid or redeemable for some *limited period of time*. The table below shows some common language used to promote these offers.

Type of Deal	Common Language
Discount	"Get 20% this week only"
Flash sale	"50% off liquidation sale—everything must go!"
Rebate	"Get a $50 rebate when purchasing online. Redeemable until the end of the month"
Buy something, get something else	"Buy one tractor, get one free. Valid for 12 hours only"
Refer-a-friend	"Special holiday offer: earn store credit when you tell your friends about us"
Frequent shopper program	"Get a free coffee after eight purchases"
Free samples or trial offers	"Try it for free while supplies last"
Randomized discount	"Spin the wheel and see how much you save"
Contests	"Enter now and win big"

Observe how your own behavior can change when confronted with incentives. Did you really need that jumbo-sized carton of jelly beans? Probably not . . . but *it was on sale*. There's a more convenient flight on another airline . . . but if you fly with your usual carrier, you'll earn more points. Maybe you don't like that coffee shop as much as the other one . . . but you're only two stamps away from a free mocha!

If you're immune to such behavior, congratulations. Just remember that most of us aren't, so as you build your hustle, don't forget about the tank you have sitting in your backyard.

THE PSYCHOLOGY OF SCARCITY AND URGENCY

You don't have to know exactly how or why this works; you just need to know that it does. Unless you're incredibly disciplined, you can see it in your own spending patterns.

But if you're interested, here's a *very quick* rundown on why all of us are conditioned to respond to sales and special offers. Two key psychological variables are at work: scarcity and urgency. The first relates to the perception of limited resources or opportunities, and the second relates to the perception that those resources or opportunities won't be around forever.

SCARCITY: "There are only a limited number of items! I'll miss out if I don't buy one."

URGENCY: "The deal is going to go away soon. I'll miss out if I don't buy it *now*."

Generally speaking, the more you can introduce these factors in your marketing—without being dishonest—the more successful you'll be. It doesn't have to seem "salesy"—find the approach that's best for you.

DON'T BE A COPYCAT

When it comes to these kinds of offers, it pays to think outside the box. In *The $100 Startup*, I told a story of two guys, Adam and Karol, who started a "fire sale" consisting of a bundle of popular digital products. They called it Only 72, referring to the fact that the sales would last for seventy-two hours only before disappearing forever. This project was a huge success, producing income of multiple six figures before the founders moved on to other projects.

Adam and Karol weren't the first to produce this kind of sale, but it wasn't common in their field at the time, and they did it in a unique way—that's why it worked.

Then came all the copycats. As someone who tends to get himself on all kinds of mailing lists for this sort of thing (whether I sign up or not) my inbox was filled with repeated pitches each week: "I'm doing a bundle sale. Want to be part of it?" Pretty soon my default answer went from "That sounds interesting, tell me more" to "No thanks." Some of the other sales produced decent results, but because they had become so unoriginal, few (if any) were as profitable as Only 72.

It reminded me of the story of the Million Dollar Homepage. In the early days of the Internet, a British student named Alex Tew had the crazy idea to sell one million dollars' worth of ad space on a site consisting of a single page.

Like a lot of crazy ideas, it worked—partly because it sounded ridiculous, and partly because Alex was able to generate a flurry of media hits, largely thanks to being first to think up such an improbable concept.[*]

Following Alex's success, numerous other sites popped up with

---

[*] According to Wikipedia, Alex raised a total of $1,037,100 in advertising revenue.

the same promise. As you might guess, these "me too" gimmicks received far less attention, from either the media and from potential sponsors.

If you're ever tempted to copy someone else's model, remember that the next clever tactic is still waiting to be discovered. Will you be the one to find it?

GUIDELINES, TIPS, AND TRICKS

Special offers are more of an art than a science, but a few simple guidelines may help.

1. ANNOUNCE THE SALE IN ADVANCE.

Don't just show up with a sale; let people know that it's coming. You don't have to give them all the details, but creating anticipation can go a long way toward creating an eager crowd of buyers just waiting to burst through the door when your sale starts.

2. YOUR CUSTOMERS SHOULDN'T HAVE TO JUMP THROUGH A BUNCH OF HOOPS TO TAKE ADVANTAGE OF THE DEAL.

A hair salon in my neighborhood regularly advertises a deal: "Tell your friends about us! If they mention you during their visit, you'll earn 25 percent off one full-priced haircut." This might sound like a decent deal, but consider the process: first, you have to put your credibility on the line in referring your friends to the salon. Then, you have to remind them to specifically mention you, or apparently you don't get the deal. That's a lot of pressure!

3. THE SALE MUST PROVIDE SUBSTANTIAL PERCEIVED SAVINGS FOR CUSTOMERS.

Imagine the above deal, only this time you'll merely save 10 percent. Oh, and remember, you can only take the savings on a full-priced haircut. If haircuts are discounted for any other reason, forget about the 10 percent savings. Uninspiring, right?

4. MAKE SURE YOU PROVIDE AN OFFER THAT CUSTOMERS CAN GET EXCITED ABOUT.

The key here is to appeal to emotion and show them why they simply must have something they may not even have realized they wanted. Ideally, you want them to think, *Wow, that's an amazing offer. Maybe I really* do *need a carton of jelly beans!*

5. TEST YOUR SYSTEMS (ORDER FORM, SHOPPING CART, ETC.) TO MAKE SURE EVERYTHING REFLECTS THE RIGHT INFO.

You'll probably have to change some settings and copy on your website when you offer a sale. Before you send a flood of interested prospects to your online home (or retail location), make sure everything is consistent and works as it should! There's nothing worse than when customers think they're getting a great deal, only to find out the discount or offer doesn't automatically get applied at checkout like the ad promised.

6. WHEN THE SALE ENDS, IT REALLY ENDS.

People will often ask you to extend the sale for them. Most of the time, the best policy is to say no. You said the sale ended at a certain time, so if you make exceptions for people, you're not only calling your credibility into question, you're breaking your word to everyone else. A brief grace period is fine, but for the most part you should hold fast to your principles. By doing so, they'll be much more likely to pay attention and not miss out the next time.

When Andrew and I last talked, he was on track to making more than $25,000 from the slate project thus far. For him, the 20 percent offer not only led to an influx of sales, it also expanded his pool of customers. That's another benefit to this strategy: when people buy from you at a discount and walk away satisfied with the product, they're more likely to come back and buy more from you again *and* tell their friends about the experience.

Not only is Andrew $25,000 richer, he's also excited about the future and has an ambitious plan to expand his hustle to replace his full-time engineering salary. And all this has happened without his making any real investment into marketing. As a side benefit, he never has to buy another birthday, wedding, or housewarming present again—he just makes a custom slate piece, then wraps a bow on it for an instant and unforgettable gift.

If you forget everything else from this section, remember this: to make more money, offer a limited time discount or a sale. Show up in a tank!

Frame Your First Dollar

> Always celebrate your early achievements.
> There's more work to be done, but small victories
> can be disproportionately satisfying.

When Max Robinson of Scotland opened the email telling him he'd be receiving a $200 check in the mail, he thought it should have gone to his spam folder. A week later, when he received the actual check, he first had to look up the currency exchange rate to figure out what it was worth in his country. He worried it wouldn't go through when he deposited it at the bank—but happily, the payment cleared.

The money had arrived from his new friends at Amazon.com. He'd never actually met these friends; he'd just signed up for the company's revenue-sharing program on a whim. It all started when he built a website dedicated to his unique hobby during some downtime from his job as the owner of a construction company. His hobby was fish, and specifically, fish tanks.

He wrote up a few interesting reviews of fish tanks (yes, they really are interesting—I'll get to that) and posted them on the site, along with links to purchase various models on Amazon. Then, after a few late nights getting the project set up, things got busy at work and he forgot about it for a while.

Seeing the email three weeks later, and then the check, and then the money in the bank, got his mind back on it. Had he really made $200 just for writing reviews of fish tanks? Indeed he had. His partner didn't believe it at first either—at least until he took her to a nice dinner with the money.

The $200 felt special to Max. In his construction company, he regularly dealt in much larger amounts of money. But for him, and for many others in the world of side hustles, those earnings were about more than the money, they were about pride. They reflected the joy of looking at that check and thinking: *I made that*.

The other great thing about that initial payment was the promise of future ones. He hadn't done anything special to market the site. He'd even abandoned it as he focused on his construction duties. Would those new friends at Amazon.com send him a check again next month, and what about the month after that? Also, what would happen if he put more effort into the work—if he wrote more fish tank reviews, would he make more money?

These questions were intriguing, and Max longed to explore them. But it all started with that first commission check. It wasn't just spending money, it was a down payment on possibility.

INVEST IN YOURSELF

All over the world, restaurant and shop owners are in the habit of framing their first dollar. You see it behind the cash register or on the wall next to worn-out newspaper clippings of reviews or other memorabilia. Sometimes there's a story that goes along with it, and sometimes there's just the dollar. It might not be an actual dollar, of course—maybe it's a photo of their first customer, or one of the owner standing behind the counter on the day the store first opened. Whatever it is, it communicates a message of pride and ownership: "We did this!"

Side hustler, you need a place to frame your dollar.

Making money for yourself, outside of your day job, is a transformative experience. Over and over I've seen how empowering it can be, especially for people who've always worked traditional jobs and haven't ever struck out on their own.

That's why it's important to celebrate the achievement somehow, even if you don't literally frame your first dollar. Max had the great idea of taking his partner out for a nice dinner. That way, he could share the celebration with her—and it also helped her to become more supportive of the project.

In almost every story featured in this book, the person behind the story spoke to me about the joy they experienced upon realizing that their hustle was working. In many cases, the intangible benefits exceeded the very tangible benefit of, well, making more money.

When you work for a company, one way or another you make your employer a lot more money than you are paid. That's not a bad thing—it's how the world works, and if your employer didn't make money, both of you would be in trouble. But that's also why side hustles are so important. You can recapture some of that value for yourself.

When you're first hustling, it's good to be frugal and conservative. You want to keep expenses low and focus on growing income. But don't take this too far. Your hustle exists to pay you, not the other way around. Don't just invest back in "the business." Invest in yourself. What's on your bucket list? Is there a trip you've always wanted to take?

Even small celebrations can be meaningful. Go to a new restaurant that might normally be out of your budget or comfort zone. Get a massage. Take an afternoon off and spend it browsing at the bookstore or going to the movies. Take the win—you deserve it.

———

After Max's unexpected $200 surprise, he resumed work on the project. He wrote more reviews, updated the pages, and filled out the content a bit more. Within a few months, he was regularly earning an average of $700 each month, without adding anything to the site or otherwise doing anything at all. It really is a "set it and forget about it" hustle. Like some of the others you've read about, it probably won't last forever, but that's okay. In the meantime, it's allowed him to take two extra vacations a year.

Because Max is based in the United Kingdom, he had the option to take his commissions via direct deposit to his bank account. He declined that option, though—he *liked* the physical check coming in the mail every month. It was fun, and he feels the same surge of pride each time it arrives. He might try to start more projects like the fish tank blog, or he might remain focused on his construction company, or he might do something totally different—but no matter what, the unexpected success has made a major, positive difference in his life.

Your hustle can bring you the same surge of confidence and pride. As soon as you have something to celebrate, even a minor victory, take the win. *You did this.*

WEEK 4 RECAP!

Your offer is out in the world! There's more to be done, but there's also much to celebrate.

— KEY POINTS —

- Start before you're ready and look for "proof of concept."

- "Sell like a Girl Scout"—if you've correctly identified your ideal customer, remember that they're looking

for you, not just the other way around. Don't be
afraid to get creative in reaching them with your
message.

- Testing is boring in the way that making a lot of
  money is boring. Set up at least one A/B test to see
  how you can improve your offer.

- Use deals and promotions to encourage action. Show
  up with a tank!

WEEK 4: LAUNCH YOUR IDEA
TO THE RIGHT PEOPLE

Day 17: Publish Your Offer!   ✓

Day 18: Sell Like a Girl Scout   ✓

Day 19: Ask Ten People for Help   ✓

Day 20: Test, Test, and Test Again   ✓

Day 21: Burn Down the Furniture Store ✓

Day 22: Frame Your First Dollar   ✓

REGROUP AND REFINE

Your hustle is out in the world!
Congratulations—now let's see what you can
do to raise the game.

WEEK 5: REGROUP AND REFINE

Day 23: Track Your Progress and
Decide on Next Steps

Day 24: Grow What Works,
Let Go of What Doesn't

Day 25: Look for Money Lying Under
a Rock

Day 26: Get It Out of Your Head

Day 27: Back to the Future

Track Your Progress and Decide on Next Steps

> As you learn more about how customers respond
> to your hustle, take note of the most crucial
> metrics—then take action on what you learn.

When Tim Aton was just a sophomore in high school, he aspired to work as a programmer for a digital agency. Being a high school student, he knew he had to do something to stand out—so he decided to create an unconventional résumé. Instead of using a word processor like most people would, he used Adobe's Photoshop suite to create a visual résumé that looked totally different from every normal résumé he'd ever seen. He didn't end up getting a job, perhaps because he was just fifteen years old, but the agency's owner took notice and became a mentor to him.

A few years later, he remembered this experience when he was in college and needed to make some cash. Maybe, he thought, he could offer a custom résumé service for other students. Tim was smart and didn't want to limit his customer pool to just students at his college—he knew the potential market was much larger. He decided to promote the offer online. He went to the website Fiverr .com and posted a listing: "I will create a stunning custom résumé for $5."

That very first day he received an order, and once he filled it and received a rave review, more began to follow, and within a few short weeks he was receiving and filling more than eight orders a day. Five dollars an order won't take you far, but Tim was smart. Even though basic services on Fiverr cost just $5, the site lets you offer a lot of upgrades and cross-sells in your listing. By adding on some additional purchase options, Tim's average order tripled to $15. Still, this wasn't a ton of money, and he was a busy student who had to budget his time carefully. Once his class schedule filled up, he shut down the listing.

At the end of the next term, however, he returned to the idea. He felt he was on to something with the idea of résumé templates. They were interesting, fun, and clearly a lot of people liked them. From all those orders on Fiverr, he knew there was a clear demand. But he also knew that he didn't want to spend all his time filling custom orders for small amounts of money. Could there be a better way?

Tim spent part of the next summer trying a few different ideas. First, he listed his offer on a different website, trying to break free of the Fiverr ecosystem where low prices ruled the day. The results were lackluster, but he still believed in the concept. Then, he tried creating his own website, Résumé Redesign. But this didn't quite get off the ground either.

Finally, more than a year after he'd filled his first order, he realized something. He didn't want to be a designer doing client work, creating visual résumés one at a time, from scratch. What he wanted to do was sell a template. He called the new business Foundry Resumes, and he created sixteen unique designs. It was a lot of work to create so many templates, but *template* is the key word: once he made them, they didn't need to be changed or customized, or at least not by him. Tim would sell the templates, and customers would personalize them on their own time.

By switching from selling custom designs to selling a template, he was also switching from a service-based hustle to a product-based one. For this new focus, Tim created a new website. He also listed the templates for sale on Creative Market, a directory of design assets and stock photos that people pay to download.

Just as when he first launched his original service two years earlier, he had sales coming in right from the beginning. This time, he sold the templates for $11 instead of $5, and he no longer had to do any work to fulfill the orders. Instead of looking at his inbox and feeling overwhelmed every morning, he looked at his checking account and saw money coming in on a regular basis. Within a few months, this side hustle was earning more than $450 a month.

MEASURE YOUR ORIGINAL IDEA: IS IT WORKING?

When you ask many business owners how their business is going, they tend to say things like "Oh, it's fine." Whether they're making a million dollars a week or nearly bankrupt, the response is always the same. But a business is never doing "fine." Maybe it's succeeding or maybe it's not, but it's on a trajectory one way or another.

In the early stages of your hustle, you need to be able to answer an important question, "Is it working?," with something other than "Oh, it's fine." You must objectively evaluate your hustle, and be honest with yourself about whether it's actually making money or not. When you ask, "Is it working?," there are only three possible outcomes.

OUTCOME 1: *You're crushing it!* Initial results are way above your back-of-napkin projections. The bank has called to make sure you aren't selling drugs or laundering money. You're thrilled to be riding this train, and you're excited to see what comes next.

OUTCOME 2: *Womp-womp.* You had a good idea, but it hasn't panned out. Instead of a stampede of buyers, when you opened the doors, you found yourself standing alone in the middle of an empty shop.

These two outcomes each present a clear next step: if it's working, great—keep doing it. If it's not, well, you need to cut your losses and try something else. But it's just as likely, if not more so, that you'll experience a third outcome.

OUTCOME 3: *Your idea works, sort of.* In this very common outcome, your hustle hasn't made a lot of money yet, but you still feel good about the direction. There's been enough early interest to make you confident that with some refining (see Day 25) and the help of a few friends (see Day 19), sales will pick up. Or maybe it's the opposite—you've had a few sales and earned some cash, but you no longer feel that this hustle is right for you.

Most of the time, your experience will fall in this category, and that's okay. If you've followed the steps in this book, you're unlikely to fall flat on your face. But many profitable ideas aren't huge successes right out of the gate, either. Knowing what to do *after* debuting a hustle will make a huge difference in your long-term results. How do you know what to do next? You look at metrics. The data will help you decide.

TRACK WHAT MATTERS, IGNORE WHAT DOESN'T

On Day 20, you learned about testing. In a way, tracking data is a more advanced form of testing, yet it doesn't need to be complicated. Giant businesses like Amazon.com track dozens or even hundreds of metrics. But remember, you're not Amazon.com—so don't do that. You just need to monitor a couple of important numbers that will make a real difference in your long-term results.

Think about how you track other things in your life, including your health and personal finance. At any given time, do you have an approximate idea of how much money is in your checking account? (Most people do.) What about your health—how do you feel right now? (It's another easy question.) For each of these areas you could collect all sorts of other data, but by answering these two simple questions the big picture is easy to discern.

That's how it should be with your hustle: at any given time, you should know its general health and well-being. This isn't hard when you keep up with your metrics in three key areas:

- Profit (income minus expenses)

- Growth (number of new prospects, customers, or clients)

- Time (how many hours per week you spend starting and operating the project)*

As part of tracking growth, you may also want to look at website analytics (statistics) to see who's visiting your site and where they're coming from. Again, this doesn't need to be complicated. I use a very simple spreadsheet to keep up with most of my hustles. It's a lot like the back-of-the-napkin projection method you learned on Day 5, except instead of expenses and income, you want to track the key metrics I mentioned above.†

There may be other metrics that are relevant to your hustle, and it's fine to keep an eye on them. Just be careful to avoid becoming obsessed with data that doesn't affect your profit or growth.

---

* In the long term, it's good to know your approximate "hourly wage" for what you earn on your hustle. But you may want to separate startup time from operation time, since startup time is highly variable.

† *Profit First* by Mike Michalowicz is a great book that provides an alternative means of tracking growth. Mike's theory is that most of us are used to looking at our bank balance, so we should build a tracking system around that habit.

IF AT FIRST YOU ~~DON'T~~ SUCCEED, KEEP TRYING

Tim could have kept running himself ragged making custom résumés for $5, and it technically would have been a viable hustle. But while it was a great experiment and helped him gain confidence in his skills, he also knew it was a bad idea in the long run.

His results indicated he was in Outcome 3 territory, where the initial idea worked, *sort of.* But when he reviewed his key metrics, especially the time he was spending to fulfill each low-priced order, he realized that for his side hustle to be sustainable for the long term, he'd have to change his approach. Due to the demand that he had seen, he still believed that the core problem he was trying to solve was the right one. He would just need to change the solution he provided for it.

ORIGINAL STRATEGY

PROBLEM: Résumés are boring.

SOLUTION: Offer custom, visually appealing résumés on demand.

REVISED STRATEGY

PROBLEM: Résumés are boring.

SOLUTION: Offer a series of résumé templates for sale, allowing customers to do their own customization.

The new approach allowed Tim to serve more customers *and* free up more of his time, while still getting paid. This was a major victory, and it enabled him to put the business on autopilot as he worked on other hustles.

DECIDE ON NEXT ACTIONS

You've diligently followed the program, and now your hustle is out in the world. You've tested it out with customers, and by now you should have some conclusive data on how well it's working.

As you review your initial results, try to get as objective a view as possible. At this juncture, you need to make a big decision: abandon ship and try something else, or stay the course and adjust your sails. All the steps in this week assume that you're choosing door number two. You're continuing with the project, but improving it to make more money, take less time, become more sustainable, or achieve some other goal. If you're choosing door number one, that's okay, but before you can raise your game—the main goal of this week—you'll need to jump back to the beginning of the program and create a new hustle.

At the end of the day, you're really just looking to answer one simple question: Is your hustle profitable? Yes, there's more than one way to measure success, but your side hustle *should* make money. If your business gained a hundred more social media followers this week, that's great—but you can't deposit those people in your bank account. Expect your hustle to give you the results you want, or choose a different hustle.

Oh, and just to make things fun, there's another potential scenario: at your period of first evaluation, you may find that your hustle is working, *but* you've reached maximum output for this particular project. For example, if you've built a treehouse in your backyard and are renting it out on Airbnb, you probably can't build *another* one. So in that case, you may simply choose to let the treehouse keep producing income (remember, money grows on trees . . .) while you spend your free time on hobbies or family.

Chances are, though, once you're hooked on hustling, you'll probably want another project. If you've reached maximum output, simply go back to the list of ideas you put together when we started, or come up with a new idea entirely. Now that you're an experienced side hustler, you probably have no shortage of ideas and should have no trouble getting one of them off the ground.

With his unconventional résumé service turned product, Tim had effectively built a treehouse in his backyard—the project had fulfilled its goal and was now working hard to earn passive income for him. He could have kept working on it in hopes of growing it further, but instead he looked to the future and decided to pursue one of his many other ideas. That's the great thing about side hustles: once you get started making money, it's hard to stop!

DAY 24

Grow What Works, Let Go of What Doesn't

> As your hustle grows, there are countless
> options to expand. Don't get distracted—
> identify what's working and do more of that.

Ana Ramirez had worked in marketing for most of her career. One day, without much warning, her San Diego company restructured and she was downsized. Looking back, she calls it a blessing in disguise. Around that time, her mother became terminally ill. Being out of work allowed Ana to spend those last few months by her side.

In one of their extended conversations, her mother made a suggestion: Why don't you try selling your art? In addition to being an experienced marketer, Ana was also a talented photographer. In her marketing job, she had become familiar with stock photo sites, where businesses went to purchase images for commercial projects. She knew that most of the bigger sites worked with lots of independent photographers, who uploaded batches of images and made a cut each time one of their photos was purchased and downloaded from the stock site.

She'd also found websites that would allow artists to upload their images to be printed and shipped to customers, with the revenue being split in some fashion between the artist and the company that provides the platform. For Ana, this was more appealing than the stock photo sites—she loved the idea that her art would be featured in homes all over the country and increasingly around the world. Still, she tried out both options, experimenting with different ways of selling art instead of committing to just one.

It turned out that although the major stock sites got an enormous amount of traffic, they also hosted an enormous number of images. This meant that while the customer pool was large, the chances of any given customer actually coming across one of Ana's photos was small. On the other end of the spectrum, the sites that produced and shipped beautiful physical prints didn't get a whole lot of visitors. There, too, her work just wasn't getting in front of enough potential customers.

One day, she got an email from someone who worked for Pottery Barn—they'd come across her photography and wanted to market it to their huge customer base. Ana was thrilled when they licensed several prints and began selling them in stores and online.

Once this major national brand started carrying her work, Ana had far more exposure to far more customers than she could have reached on her own, and the hustle now brings in about a third of her total income. She's back to working in marketing to pay the rest of her bills, but her goal is to flip that equation so that the hustle brings in at least two-thirds of what she needs to live on.

FIND THE WINNERS AND FOCUS ON THEM

After you've reviewed your initial results and made some decisions about your next steps, you need to get back to work. What you do at this juncture can make a huge difference in the long-term success of your hustle.

Let's assume you decided, based on the data you looked at in the last chapter, to continue to adjust and improve upon your current hustle. The next decision you have to make is: *What* will you adjust and *how* will you improve?

Often, the answer comes down to your offer itself. For example, if you've offered three items for sale and one of them is doing much better than the others, you should probably devote your attention to *further increasing* the sales of the bestselling item. This may seem counterintuitive—you might be tempted to think it's better to try bringing the others up to the same level of sales as the winner. I struggle with this, too, and have to regularly remind myself of the "winners take all" principle as I choose between different projects. But keep in mind that you've offered people three things and they've clearly favored one of them. Why spend your limited time pushing something else?

Similarly, if you tried something that sank like a stone, it's okay to let it go—throwing things out is part of the hustler's journey. Average is boring. Find the winners and focus your efforts on them.

THE POWER OF ITERATION

Regrouping and refining are the superhero skills of side hustle success. Consider this quote from Bill Gates: "Headlines are misleading. Bad news is a headline, and gradual improvement is not." Tracking, testing, and refining are all about achieving gradual improvement. You might not make a lot of fanfare when you gradually improve an existing hustle, but you'll probably make more money.

Iteration means "the act of repeating a process," usually with the goal of improving each step along the way. As you continue to develop and improve your hustle, follow these two basic rules of iteration:

1. If it works, do more of it.

2. If it doesn't work, abandon it and move on.

Again, this is counterintuitive for many of us. It's human nature to try to fix a situation that isn't working or believe that if you just stick it out, good things will eventually happen. I often look at people who are more successful than me to see what they're doing differently. After acknowledging my envy and choosing to be grateful for all that I have, I tend to notice something they have in common. It may not have happened right away, but over time they've found what works best for them . . . and then they do more of that thing.

EMBARRASSING PERSONAL STORY

Allow me to tell you a highly embarrassing personal story. I'd love to say this is someone else's embarrassing anecdote, but sadly it's not. Very early in my entrepreneurial career, I made a big mistake. I heard about a business opportunity that promised to pay big returns, if only I'd invest $2,000 up front and wait at least three months to get anything back. If that sounds like a bad idea, well, that's because it was. In my naïveté, though, probably coupled with a certain amount of greed, I didn't see through the charade. I sent in a $2,000 check, which was a very large amount of money for me at the time. Then I waited, and then I waited some more. After three months, I hadn't seen a dime. Another three months went by, and I started getting checks in the mail, but for very small amounts.

It took me more than a year to admit to myself that I'd been fooled. Aside from those small checks, which in the end totaled less than $30, I never saw any of the original investment again.

I don't look back on this story and feel triumphant about all I've learned since then. In fact, I still feel bad about it. I remember wasting money I didn't have during a time I really couldn't afford to waste it. But the one thing I'm glad about is that even though it took me longer than it should have, I finally gave up obsessing about it and started working on other projects. If I hadn't, I'd have continued to remain stuck, waiting on something that was clearly not going to happen.

Don't make the mistake I did. If you're sitting around waiting for a payday that is clearly never going to arrive, get yourself unstuck and move on.

AUDIT YOUR SIDE HUSTLE

In my last book, I wrote about an exercise called the "Mo' Money" day, where you take a day once a quarter to focus on things you can do to make more money. Here's an updated version that focuses on side hustles.

Every month or two, take a step back and have a conversation with yourself. Ask yourself specific, open-ended questions about how things are going. These might help:

- What's working well with this hustle, and how can I develop that (or those things) further?

- Is there anything about this hustle that I could automate or outsource?

- What could I do to make more money without spending a great deal more time?

- Could I increase the price of the offer(s) associated with this hustle?

After conducting your audit, set goals based on what you've learned. For example, if you determine that you have some room to raise your prices, start with a 5 percent increase for now and decide to review the results after a certain period of time. Gradual improvement may not make for a great headline, but it looks great when you deposit it in your bank account.

REGROUP TO WIN

Some of the best stories I've heard come from people whose first attempt at a hustle failed to produce stellar results—but then they regrouped and came away much stronger with the next effort. These people didn't give up, at least not permanently. They knew that sometimes it takes more than one attempt to get it right. But they also didn't just wait around hoping more money would magically fall from the sky (like I did in my embarrassing story), either. Instead, they hustled.

And even when you do have an immediate hit, continuous improvement can usually make it much better. We're all on a journey, and tweaking as you go along is how you win. If something you've tried has started off strong, pay attention and see how you can improve it further. Set a goal to do *one thing* that will increase income in the existing hustle. Similarly, don't be afraid to let go of at least one thing that isn't working well, and then put that energy toward improving the things that are.

Look for Money Lying Under a Rock

> One of the easiest ways to grow a hustle
> is by horizontal expansion. If everything's
> going well, consider adding another version
> of it to better serve your customers.

Trevor Mountcastle's first side hustle had nothing to do with making money—or at least, money wasn't the goal. By day, Trevor is a senior program analyst supporting the federal government. In his off hours, he's an avid Frequent Flyer and "travel hacker," always on the lookout for creative strategies to earn more points and miles. A few years ago, he discovered a way to buy gift cards on one website, then buy electronic items on another site to resell at equal value. It may sound like a lot of work for not a whole lot of profit, but a valuable reward was attached to it: the credit card points and miles he earned allowed him and his wife to see more than forty countries, often in first class. He even took his dad and brother around the whole world, visiting Dubai, Singapore, and Sydney—all on miles.

A funny thing happened on the way to Trevor's next airfare upgrade: he started making money. His original goal was just to break even on his arbitrage operation, selling the items he purchased for close to the same price. But the more items he bought to resell, the better he became at knowing when he could command a higher price.

Soon, in addition to the miles and points, he was also making a tidy profit. He began expanding his operation further, visiting retail stores to buy bulk items, then sending them to a warehouse where they'd be reshipped to shoppers who purchased online. The work involves lots of tracking and spreadsheets, but Trevor finds it fun. Most of his profit margins are relatively small (he sells a lot of items, so the money adds up), but once in a while he hits on something that brings in a lot of income at once.

The first year of the hustle, he earned around $5,000. Each year after that, he's either doubled or tripled that figure, to the point where it now brings in more than $100,000 a year exclusively from his hustle. Naturally, he still travels, and because he never touches most of his inventory (all of his orders are shipped out by Amazon .com), the hustle keeps humming along—even while he's sipping champagne at thirty thousand feet.

BUY LOW, SELL HIGH

In the classic *Oregon Trail* game, a wagon full of pioneers sets out to travel from Independence, Missouri, to the West Coast wilderness. Along the way, they're beset with numerous obstacles: disease, attack from bandits, environmental hardships. The goal of the game is to soldier through the challenges and eventually arrive at a faraway settlement with as many members of your party as you can. When starting out, you receive a small amount of money that you can use to purchase supplies such as oxen, clothes, and ammunition for hunting. Then, along the way you have the opportunity to restock from general stores and itinerant merchants.

Most players try to ration their supplies as best they can and try to make their money last the whole journey to Willamette Valley.

But what many don't realize is that you can buy *and* sell from the merchants you encounter, and naturally the price is different from place to place. Smart players will follow the classic advice for picking stocks: buy low, sell high.

Trevor's side hustle is a real-life *Oregon Trail*. He attempts to buy low and sell high. Sometimes he hits the jackpot with a big profit margin. Other times, he gets stuck with an item that doesn't resell—basically a natural risk of the business. But by constantly experimenting with his inventory and prices, he's able to continuously eke out consistent profits, along with all those points and miles he uses to travel in style with his family.

A SIDE HUSTLE IS DIFFERENT FROM OTHER BUSINESSES

In the beginning of the book, I mentioned that opportunities to hustle are everywhere. By using the power of observation to identify ideas, then applying the business knowledge you've learned, you'll be able to set up new hustles on a regular basis—or you can simply focus on fine-tuning your first one to make more money, just like Trevor did.

There's a school of thought that advises you to focus on making money only from one revenue source or only on offers that are fully aligned with your core business. This conventional "wisdom" is commonly taught in business school, business books, and executive coaching. But the side hustler's mindset is different, or at least it should be. After all, it's something you're doing on the side. You aren't trying to build a Silicon Valley startup and make money for a million investors; you're doing this to make money for yourself.

Consider the Million Dollar Homepage, started by a college student, that I mentioned on Day 21. The traditional business perspective would argue that such a thing is a gimmick, and a distraction from some "real" business that he could have been building. This is, of course, terrible advice. If you happen to find a million dollars lying under a rock somewhere, *pick it up.*

LET'S TURN OVER SOME ROCKS!

For a lot of businesses, it's generally much easier to sell more to existing customers than it is to acquire new ones. Yet most business owners (not just side hustlers, but also full-time entrepreneurs) cast their gaze toward growth by customer acquisition alone. This is a big mistake.

The easiest way to turn over a rock and sell more to your current customers is to "remix" your offer.

To remix, you typically add an additional version of what you're already doing. Maybe it's a premium version, a "next-level" version, a Volume II—or something else entirely. If your side hustle is a service, you want to find a way to offer another service that complements the first one. If it's a product, you should ask yourself what other related or complementary products you could add.

Say you're a language tutor who's compiled a great method for helping people brush up their Spanish. Your method is called "Speak Spanish by 4 p.m." With this kind of hustle, the additional products you could sell are numerous, if not nearly unlimited. You could:

- Offer the same method in an all-new language ("Speak French by 4 p.m.")

- Offer an intermediate or advanced version of the method ("Speak Fluently by Sunset")

- Upsell customers with a special "4 p.m. vocabulary kit" that helps them learn more words in a short period of time

- Offer individualized coaching to go along with the proven method

- Offer the method in a different format than the original one (if the original format was audio, make a video version; if the original format was an e-book, produce a course)

The point is that once you know that people like what you're selling, it's not usually difficult to figure out how to expand your offerings. Let's look at a couple of examples from hustlers you've read about in previous chapters.

THE SLATE MASON. Andrew Church in Pennsylvania had always been good with his hands. He carved his last name out of slate and hung it up in his house, where visitors frequently commented on how nice it looked. Then he decided to chisel the shape of his home state into another handcrafted item, and this time he put it on etsy for sale. Within just a few days, he'd sold several pieces, so he knew it was a viable concept. The expansion idea was obvious: news reports indicate that Pennsylvania is only one of fifty states! He got to work creating designs for the other forty-nine and now sells them nationwide.*

THE PROGRAMMER. Dan Khadem worked as a database programmer for a Denver hospital. He started tutoring students and other professionals in Microsoft Access, a powerful (yet difficult to master) software program. Tutoring worked well, and he was able to charge $55 an hour for several hours of sessions each week. But he also noticed that some of his students had additional needs that were more

---

* It's more than a metaphor: Andrew is literally finding money under a rock.

complex. In some cases, the companies they worked for required custom database work, so Dan took that on, too—and was able to bump his rates up to $85–$110 an hour.

These examples may get you thinking. In almost every side hustle, there are numerous opportunities to branch out without expending a ton of effort. You've already found a way to make money by making something that people want. What can you make for them *next*?

The answer to that question will help you decide on an additional version or companion project for your side hustle.

GIVE PEOPLE A CHOICE, SORT OF

When you remix your offer, you're also providing a choice of options. This can be good *or* bad. *Too* much choice and the customer feels confused and overwhelmed. Some choice, however, is usually smart.

In addition to providing options, giving people a choice is also a marketing tactic—either an evil one or a genius one, or maybe an evil genius one depending on your perspective. When a savvy marketer presents a choice, they try to do so in a way that makes it hard to say no:

"Will that be cash or credit?"
"Do you want to pay now or later?"
"Which version would you like to purchase?"

Notice that in none of these scenarios is there an easy option to say "No, thanks."

To be fair, those questions are a bit exaggerated—you really *don't* want people to buy something out of undue pressure. They won't be happy in the end, and you might not sleep well at night. Still, this kind of marketing isn't always evil. The reality is that people want at least some choice. Give the people what they want!

If Trevor had stuck to reselling as a hobby, he wouldn't be making money now. Once he realized he could profit from his arbitrage efforts, he invested more time and energy in finding more and more opportunities and buying more and more products to resell. Of course, even though he's now making "real money," he still receives the original benefit of all those points and miles. He recently returned from yet another trip around the world—in first class, of course. And the whole time he was flying high, he continued to receive new deposits of cash in his bank account.

Get It Out of Your Head

> Every business has key systems. As a side hustler,
> yours are probably stored in your head—and
> that's not always wise. To make significant
> improvements (and save more time) as you expand
> your hustle, systemize wherever you can.

Serial hustler Adam White had several projects competing for his attention. There was the day job as director of digital marketing for a charter bus company. There was the film he was making at night and on weekends, and the young adult novel he tried to make progress on each morning before leaving for the office. By now you know how this works: busy people are good at side hustles, because they know how to make their time count.

As part of his day job, he spent a lot of time doing promotion through guest posts on business blogs. The process was time-consuming, and he had a hard time keeping up with them all. Some blogs accepted guest posts and others didn't. The ones that did usually had certain requirements that had to be followed, which weren't always consistent. Then, after submitting a post, Adam had to remember to follow up if he didn't hear back within a reasonable period of time. Procedurally, it was a bit of a nightmare.

He started to compile detailed notes on all the blogs that accepted posts, as well as a system to track his submissions (remember the classic side hustle lesson: if what you need doesn't exist, make it yourself). Before he knew it, he had a database of information on hundreds of blogs covering lots of different categories. Thus was born the idea: Why not offer his "Guest Post Tracker" to other writers with the same problem?

After putting together a simple sales page, he asked a friend to write about it in an online business forum. Right away, more than ten people signed up, paying a $49 fee. Before the end of the week, another ten payments had come through. Adam had another side project!

The interesting thing about this hustle is that it essentially promotes itself. To market it, Adam simply writes short guest posts . . . about guest posts. Each one typically brings in another batch of customers right away, as well as an ongoing stream of customers who find the post over time.

Ninety days in, Guest Post Tracker was bringing in $1,000 a month. By further systematizing the process and repeatedly testing to improve conversion using the same kind of A/B testing I wrote about on Day 20, it was soon up to $2,000 a month. Six weeks after we first talked, Adam wrote me back to say this kind of process work had helped even more: the site was now up to $3,000 a month.

The biggest challenge for Adam, as for many hustlers, is time. With the digital marketing job, the film he's making, and the novel he's writing, the guest post hustle takes a backseat to each of those commitments. Still, because his Guest Post Tracker saves him so much time at his day job, he's able to find time to work on selling that gift of time to others.

WRITE DOWN EVERYTHING YOU DO

Adam's hustle worked because it was a great idea, but he made it work a lot *better* when he applied a systems-based, process-driven approach to it. When it comes to hustling, "systems" doesn't mean fancy IT software or expensive network servers; it simply refers to all the procedures that allow you to serve customers or otherwise make money.

At some point in their journey, longtime hustlers learn an important lesson: you can do something repeatedly, or you can do something just once. They also usually find out that documenting your work does not come naturally. Frankly, most people don't want to do it—it's a future pain point, so they wait until they have to. But if you ever want to grow your hustle, or if you just want to save time, consider doing it on the front end instead. Documenting your processes gets you out of the mundane details of the day to day. It keeps you from management by inbox. It makes life easier, and it also tends to make you more money.

MAKE WORKFLOWS FOR YOUR REPEAT PROCESSES

One of the best ways to document your systems is by creating more workflows, a concept we looked at on Day 15. Recall that a workflow is any sequence of processes that shows exactly what needs to happen for any particular outcome. You learned to list out every step that needs to happen to develop an idea. These workflows, in contrast, are for existing operations. They can help you iron out problems, improve efficiency, and make it much easier to outsource or get some help on parts of your hustle as it grows or as you expand it into other things.

The two most important workflows for most hustles are *sales* and *service*. Basically, you want to document how you sell to people and how they receive what they purchase.

Adam's sales workflow was pretty simple. He'd built a basic website that described the guest post tracking service, and he made two versions of the checkout page to test which one would convert better. To bring people to the site, he wrote guest posts on different blogs. He also pitched the product to other business media for coverage. That was pretty much it—no fancy marketing strategy, no employees, and extremely low expenses. It looked like this:

His service workflow was also simple. All he had to do was make sure that buyers received access to the tracking program, that it worked, and that it was updated fairly regularly to reflect new blogs and changes in policy. There was an occasional customer service inquiry or refund request to attend to, but all that took very little time. The process looked like this:

Adam doesn't need my advice, but let's say he read yesterday's lesson and decided to create a different version of the Guest Post Tracker. The existing version is a product. People pay once for it and receive access to something he's made that contains a lot of information. Most likely, some of that information is relevant to them and some of it isn't. Now let's say the new, different version of the Guest Post Tracker that Adam decides to make is a service. You can still buy the basic version for $49, but if you want a customized version, complete with a one-hour advisory call from Adam, you can buy that for $199.

This upgraded version of the hustle requires a new service workflow, since he now has to create customized trackers, schedule calls, and deliver advice to customers. It's still fairly simple, but notice the new workflow elements:

For workflows like this, where you need to schedule calls or other meetings with customers, it's especially important to be clear on all the details. Consider this an example of a sub-workflow that focuses on something even more specific, like scheduling:

- How will the calls be scheduled?

- When will the calls be scheduled?

- What will be the frequency of the calls—just once, more than once, or whenever the customer needs?

- What will be the agenda of the calls?

- What kind of prep work will you need to do before the call?

- What kind of follow-up work will you need to do after the call?

If this sounds tedious, remember that if something is broken in even one small part of your workflow, your hustle may falter in any number of ways. Your customers may become frustrated, your potential customers may not be persuaded to purchase, and you may struggle with keeping up. Taking the time to document your systems and improve your workflows will almost always be less tedious than the damage control you'll have to do if things go awry.

ONBOARDING

Another important workflow is focused entirely on welcoming and orienting new customers. This is called *onboarding*, and it's all about helping your buyers become familiar with whatever they've just paid for. As with the service workflow, setting up a proper onboarding process helps prevent frustration, both yours and theirs. Your goal is to create a happy, reassuring journey for your customer— and help them experience the best of what your hustle has to offer. Better onboarding creates increased retention, repeat business, and referrals.

Onboarding can be done in a number of ways. One of the simplest and most common is through an email sequence that customers receive upon signing up. When you purchase something online, you'll almost always receive a confirmation message with a receipt. But much of the time, it doesn't end there. Over the next few days or weeks, you'll usually receive an additional series of messages designed to help you become familiar with the product or service and answer any questions you may have.

There are many different formats for an onboarding email series. Yours could look something like this:

MESSAGE #1, sent right after purchase: "Welcome, new customer!"

MESSAGE #2, sent the next day: "Watch this video to learn the most important elements of your new service."

MESSAGE #3, sent three days later: "These advanced features will make your life easier."

MESSAGE #4, sent a week later: "Hey, just checking in. Is everything working for you, and do you have any questions?"*

Of course, your onboarding series will differ depending on the nature or complexity of your product or service, with some requiring more detail and guidance than others. In general, though, remember that your primary goal is to make the process as pleasant and seamless for the customer as possible.

A FEW TOOLS TO IMPROVE YOUR HUSTLE

Hustles that turn into thriving small businesses eventually need a few specific tools. You may not need all these things in the beginning—remember, simple is best when you're starting out—but it's good to familiarize yourself with what they are, so that you'll know what to look for when the time comes.

CONTACT MANAGEMENT. Commonly known as CRM, for customer relationship management, this software helps you keep tabs on lots of different people. It's particularly important if you sell expensive items or services to specific contacts you build a relationship with over time. It's less important if you sell a lot of items or services to anyone who wants them.

---

* More information on this, including a complete script with ten messages, is available at SideHustleSchool.com.

Examples: HubSpot, Salesforce, Microsoft Dynamics

PROJECT MANAGEMENT. If you end up working with a designer, web developer, assistant, or anyone else, it's great to have a shared, online workspace where you can monitor the status of different tasks.

Examples: Trello, Asana, Basecamp

BOOKKEEPING. At first, you'll probably do this yourself—but whether you end up getting help or just continue on the DIY model, you'll need to track expenses and income. You can get by with a simple spreadsheet, but when the time comes to prepare your taxes, software makes it much easier.

Examples: Wave Accounting, FreshBooks, QuickBooks

PASSWORD RECORDER. We all know that you shouldn't use the same password more than once, or at least not for everything, but these days you practically need a login to turn the coffee maker on in the morning. How do you keep up with so many passwords? The simple answer is: you don't. You register with a system that generates secure passwords *and* stores them for you so you don't have to remember them.

Examples: LastPass, RoboForm, Dashlane

Adam White, the serial hustler, had correctly identified a need for a system to help him compile information on all the different blogs he was pitching. He then used his hustle skills to make a quick profit from it. The real success, however, came when he applied his skill in systemizing and A/B testing to streamline his workflows. Three thousand dollars a month is a lot more than a thousand a month— and the difference came entirely by working smart, not just hard. Now he just needed to write that YA novel.

Back to the Future

You've come to the end of the road . . .
or is it the beginning? Side hustles create
opportunity and freedom. Once you're up
and running, your options are unlimited.

Bob Bentz is a huge baseball fan. Whenever he gets the chance, he attends Phillies games at his favorite ballpark in Philadelphia. The love of the sport has transferred to his family as well, with his son and daughter both actively playing on local teams even now that they're grown up. For many years, the only holdout was Barb, Bob's wife. She didn't *dislike* the sport, but she was more interested in the social aspects, like talking with people and cheering on the team.

One day, Barb went to the game wearing a homemade white sweater with red stitching on it that looked like a baseball. Before they'd even left the parking lot to take their seats in the stands, at least ten women had approached her to ask about it. Several of them said they wanted one—where could they buy it?

Thus the Ballpark Sweaters side hustle was born. There was clearly a demand, and with Bob's frequent visits to the park (along with Barb, who was now more excited about it), they had an instant market at their fingertips, just waiting to be served.

Bob was no stranger to side hustles, having previously started a number of websites related to fantasy sports and even having hosted a weekly fifteen-minute show on ESPN radio. He'd also already been working with a virtual assistant from Bangladesh, which was convenient—to make this hustle profitable, he knew he'd need to outsource to keep down his manufacturing costs.

They started with an order of two hundred sweaters which seemed like a reasonable number. It took six weeks, but a shipping container of baseball sweaters eventually showed up at the door from China, where the assistant had arranged for them to be manufactured. They made their first—and second—sale at the very next ball game, when Barb wore the new prototype.

Within just forty-five days, they'd sold out of that initial order and placed another, making a few adjustments based on what they'd learned from the first batch. These days, the thriving hustle brings in consistent sales with minimal marketing. And the best part is, it's not just a business; it's also *fun*.

As we emailed back and forth, Bob mentioned that the Ballpark Sweaters hustle has improved his family's life in several ways. The extra money is nice, but even better than that, it's also given Bob and Barb a project to work on together. "Ballpark Barb" handles the design and administration, while "Ballpark Bob" handles the marketing. Oh, and, there are two other important benefits. First, Barb is a lot more interested in attending the games now that she has a financial incentive to do so. Second, every night they go to the stadium, they sell at least one sweater that covers their beer tab.

WHAT'S NEXT? YOU DECIDE.

Like sweaters, side hustles aren't one size fits all. You can hustle in your own way, on your own terms. If you change your mind about something as you go along, that's fine too.

If you've followed the side hustle plan from the beginning of this book, look back at what you've made and decide what happens next. Do you want to continue building this hustle on evenings and spare weekends? Is it going so well that you want to consider going "all in," eventually leaving your job to strike out on your own?

As you consider your choices, think back to the stories you've read in this book. At different points in life, people made different decisions based on their own needs and preferences. Some hustlers went all in with their projects. Jake Posko (Day 9) started his "Most Awesome Guitar Lessons in the Universe" to escape from his job at the university. The side hustle has become the job, with one key difference: he makes all the decisions.

For others, the side hustle grew to such a level that they could make a full-time income from it—but since they liked their day job, they kept doing both. Sarah Hannington's candy heart hustle (Day 11) makes more than $100,000 during the busy Valentine's Day season. But since activity during the rest of the year is much slower, she is able to continue her role as a marketing executive for a large company, which she enjoys.

Many side hustlers just use their projects as a way to make the occasional extra cash, when they have time. Oliver Asis (Day 16), the government employee who became a part-time wedding photographer after posting an ad on Craigslist, continues to work his day job for the State of California. And once a month, he takes on a wedding gig that pays at least $3,500.

No matter what you ultimately decide, the beauty of the side-hustle-as-backup-plan is that it gives you more choices. For example, when Andrew Church's employer requested that he leave his home in Pennsylvania and move to Chicago, he was faced with a difficult decision. He didn't want to uproot his life, but how could he say no? Thanks to his side hustle, he had enough income to worry a lot less about losing his job. He went back to his boss and respectfully declined the request. "Without the side gig," he said, "I wouldn't have felt nearly as confident in making that decision."

Others built their side hustle to a point where it could operate without them, and then they went off and did other things, like Tim Aton (Day 23) who designed a series of résumé templates. When we last left off, they were making $450 a month, he had completely moved on to new projects, but the side hustle continued bringing in extra cash.

For others, having a hustle helped them in different ways, like providing security through a time of life transition. After selling her restaurant, Julie Wilder (Day 18) continued building her astrology calendar hustle, with the aim of finding success in an entirely new career, becoming a market leader in something totally different, and reaching many more people. Newlyweds David and Praj (Day 10) used their hustle to create social good by importing cashmere shawls from Nepal and investing in girls' education.

Here's the thing about a good side hustle. It can help support your life, but it doesn't have to be your whole life. In fact, thanks to the project they've built, most side hustlers are able to enjoy *more* of their life.

Always remember that a hustle is different from other startup ventures or businesses. You don't have to listen to the advice of experts or follow conventional wisdom. You don't have to "scale." You don't have to hire employees or assistants, virtual or otherwise. There is no single "right way."

There's only the right way *for you*.

On Day 10 I told you about origins stories, the importance of having a reason for your hustle. Since you've made it this far, here's *my* origins story, at least as it relates to this book. I've been self-employed for my entire adult life. For as long as I can remember, freedom has been one of my highest values. I feel incredibly fortunate that I've found a way of life that allows me to write, travel, and pursue work I find meaningful. I'm motivated by starting projects that have the potential to help other people find a similar lifestyle, even if what they have in mind for themselves is different from my semi-nomadic state of being.

Before I started writing these pages, I spent a lot of time thinking about two people: April and Parker. You already know a little about them—April is the designer I mentioned early in the book who wanted to start a hustle without leaving her job and was disappointed in the business course she took at a local college. Parker is the IT manager who made $8,000 in profit from a $100 microphone.

To me, these two people represented the opportunity that awaits those who embrace the way of the side hustle. Parker was a model hustler, the kind of person whose story I wanted to hear over and over. The $8,000 he made in his first year of hustling had an immediate positive impact on his life. April had the right vision and work ethic, and I had no doubt that she could join the ranks of people like Parker. All she needed was a bit of guidance.

With these two people in mind, I decided to go all in. I started a podcast, Side Hustle School, and I committed to making an episode every single day (no breaks!) for at least a year. On this show I tell stories of people just like the ones you've read about in this book. My mission is to show that *anyone* can increase opportunities for themselves by creating another source of income, therefore creating more freedom and more ability to choose.

The more I explore the world of hustling, the more inspiring I find it to be. If I'm able to help you with your hustle, I may not be able to fly or leap tall buildings, but I'll consider myself a minor-league superhero. I won't take the credit, though—I know you'll have done all the work.

The side hustle economy is here to stay. It's a social revolution that can improve our collective well-being and broaden our cultural approach to work. From security to extra income to confidence to fun, there are many benefits to a hustle. And when you start quickly and keep costs low, there's very little risk.

What will your story be?

WEEK 5 RECAP!

The book is almost over, but the chapter that features you is just beginning. Once you start hustling, this way of life will be with you for a long time. Continue to learn, experiment, and improve. The next steps are yours!

 KEY POINTS

- Don't worry about tracking everything, but do choose two or three metrics to keep an eye on.

- Iteration is the real way to win. If at first you succeed, try something else.

- Audit your hustle to see where you can make more money, save time, or both.

WEEK 5: REGROUP AND REFINE

Day 23: Track Your Progress and Decide on Next Steps	✓
Day 24: Grow What Works, Let Go of What Doesn't	✓
Day 25: Look for Money Lying Under a Rock	✓
Day 26: Get It Out of Your Head	✓
Day 27: Back to the Future	✓

Kitchen Sink

The book is intended to be comprehensive and give you everything you need to start. Still, there's always more to learn. These resources might help.

- **SIDE HUSTLE STARTER KITS:** Brief guides to several popular hustles discussed in the book

- **HOW TO VALIDATE AN IDEA WITH $10 AND A FACEBOOK ACCOUNT:** How to use Facebook ads to get immediate feedback

- **WRITE A LETTER TO YOUR IDEAL CUSTOMER:** A template for learning more about your target market

- **BUY A RENTAL PROPERTY WITH A $1,575 DOWN PAYMENT:** A quick primer from my go-to expert on real estate hustling

- **RESOURCES AND FREE STUFF:** Various resources and referrals

Side Hustle Starter Kits

PUT YOUR COUCH OR SPARE BEDROOM ON AIRBNB!*

With more than one million listings, Airbnb has changed the way people travel all over the world. At the same time, it's also opened up a gold mine of opportunities for side hustlers. If you have any kind of space where a stranger can sleep, you may be able to publish—and make money from—it on the site. Creative students have rented out their dorm rooms over semester break. Tenants have leased additional apartments and then sublet them every single night, pocketing the difference between what they earn in nightly fees and what they pay in monthly rent. Homeowners have built tiny cottages in their backyards to house guests. In short, you don't need to be a real estate baron to profit from Airbnb. Here's all you need to know to get started:

BUSINESS MODEL: Rent your home (or part of your home) to a visitor. The process is safe because both parties' identities are verified, and a mutual rating system encourages responsible behavior.

WHY: A huge market of people are actively searching Airbnb listings every day, and the business is very easy to learn.

AVERAGE STARTUP COST: Variable.

---

* Be sure to read up on rules and regulations in your area before doing this. Some cities are more welcoming to this practice than others.

EASE OF STARTUP: Low.

LONG-TERM POTENTIAL: Medium.

SKILLS REQUIRED: Customer service (quick response time matters). Having great photos of your rental space also makes a big difference in average rental rates, so if you're not a photographer, recruit a friend to help create the initial listing.

BENEFITS: A turnkey income source. Once it's up and running, your entire responsibilities consist of responding to inquiries, welcoming guests, and dealing with any issues.

DOWNSIDES: If something goes wrong, it's up to you to fix it.

WORKFLOW:

1. Set up your rental space (apartment, spare bedroom, campsite . . .).
2. Create an Airbnb account and make a basic listing.
3. Spiff up your listing with nice photos and a fun description.
4. Set initial rates relatively low to make sure you can get quick bookings.
5. Make sure the first few stays go very well (you want your first few ratings to be very positive).
6. Improve your listing, make any adjustments, and raise your rates after you learn the ropes.
7. Create a process for responding to inquiries and welcoming guests. That's it!

CREATE A POP-UP SHOP

When I was in Kuwait recently, I wandered into a street fair that consisted entirely of temporary storefronts. These were pop-up shops, and they've sprung up all over the world. Note that there are two major kinds of pop-up shops: those organized by a particular festival or existing venue (e.g., a shopping mall) and those that are organized independently. Unless you feel confident that you can draw sufficient traffic on your own, it may be easier to jump into an existing setup.

If you're not sure whether this kind of hustle is right for you, consider these basics.

BUSINESS MODEL: Sell direct and sell immediate. Build relationships with customers.

WHY: Pop-up shops can be fun, and for buyers there's a built-in element of urgency: if you don't buy now, it won't be here tomorrow!

AVERAGE STARTUP COST: Low to medium.

EASE OF STARTUP: Medium.

LONG-TERM POTENTIAL: Variable.

SKILLS REQUIRED: Ability to be outgoing, engage passersby, and *sell.*

BENEFITS: You'll gain immediate market feedback.

DOWNSIDES: It's a non-virtual business (i.e., you need a shop), it doesn't scale, and your success is determined largely by available foot traffic.

WORKFLOW:

1. Decide if your product or service would work well in a pop-up format. Fashion accessories and chair massages are great; selling houses probably isn't.
2. Find a location and time. Again, if you're new at this, it's best to link up with an existing show.
3. Design every element of your shop, including signage and any promotional materials (good branding goes a long way with pop-up shops).
4. Think through and set up your payment system, which can be as simple as a tablet or phone equipped with a card reader.

5. Recruit at least one person to help. You don't want to miss a sale because you wandered off to the bathroom.

6. IMPORTANT: Pop-up customers love a good promotion, so never open a shop without some kind of sale.*

7. Have something special for the people who *don't* buy. Can you offer them 15 percent off if they go to your website and make a purchase within forty-eight hours of their visit?

8. Chances are, you'll learn a lot from your first pop-up experience—so if you don't make a bunch of cash, don't give up until you've made some changes based on those learnings and tried again.

CREATE AND SELL YOUR KNOWLEDGE

Do you know how to do something that other people want to do? Whether it's building a tiny house, creating your own nail pattern designs, reprogramming your car stereo, or virtually anything else, you can package your specialized knowledge into a detailed blueprint for others to purchase. The plan need not only be in written form—you can also provide video, audio, or some other medium of instruction. Once it's complete, your blueprint has the potential to become a long-term asset, earning money for as long as the topic is relevant and as long as people are willing to pay to learn about it.

BUSINESS MODEL: Create a step-by-step guide that shows customers exactly how to do something.

WHY: People want to learn, and they'll pay for the right materials.

AVERAGE STARTUP COST: Low.

---

* Remember that the words *sale, discount, special offer,* and similar can induce buying even if the price is almost the same as it usually is. Buyers love promotions!

EASE OF STARTUP: Low.

LONG-TERM POTENTIAL: Variable.

SKILLS REQUIRED: Teaching, logical thinking, and marketing (once it's written, you'll need to get the word out!).

BENEFITS: Potential for truly passive income.

DOWNSIDES: Potential consumer resistance; may be hard to compete against free resources.

WORKFLOW:

1. Identify a topic for your blueprint. The more specific, the better.
2. Write down the major challenges that others experience when trying to tackle this topic on their own.
3. Write down each step that people need to complete to follow the blueprint to success.
4. Get feedback on the blueprint by showing it to someone who's interested in the topic. Ask them what additional questions they have and which parts need further clarification.
5. Once your blueprint is close to being finalized, write a strong pitch for it, focused on the benefits that people will receive by purchasing it and following your plan (e.g., "You'll save time and money by knowing what kind of wood to buy for your treehouse").
6. Offer your blueprint for sale in your choice of marketplace: collective online hubs such as eBay or Craigslist, or directly through your own website.
7. Contact the first few buyers to make sure the purchase process went smoothly.
8. After making any necessary revisions, sit back and collect money!

SELL PHOTOGRAPHS TO STOCK PHOTO SITES

If you have a keen eye behind the camera, you might be able to monetize the images you capture—at least, if you capture the right ones. Stock photo sites (also called "microstock") list thousands of photos and other images for licensing to businesses. They get those photos from a wide range of amateur and professional photographers, who are paid a portion of the fee each time someone downloads their work. It's a tough field because so many people want to be part of it, but if you can find a unique enough angle, it can develop into a nice hustle.

BUSINESS MODEL: Take photos and upload them to stock photo sites.

WHY: Businesses have a constant need for good images, and they're willing to pay for the right ones.

AVERAGE STARTUP COST: Low (essentially $0 if you already have a nice camera).

EASE OF STARTUP: Medium.

LONG-TERM POTENTIAL: Medium.

SKILLS REQUIRED: Photography, attention to detail.

BENEFITS: Potential for passive income.

DOWNSIDES: Lots of competition, hard to stand out.

WORKFLOW:

1. Research the most popular microstock listing sites, which allow you to upload images for licensing. Each one has strengths and weaknesses, and most tend to specialize in a particular kind of photography.
2. Take *a lot* of photos. Speaking of specialization, there are two ways to win at the stock photo game: volume and uniqueness. Most of the time, choosing to specialize in a particular theme or genre is much easier than trying to be "one photographer to rule them all."

3. Pay attention to which photographs are purchased the most. Natural, candid images of people tend to do particularly well.

4. Pay attention to which photographs are missing. If you're able to do something *really* unique—polar bears in the Arctic, for example—that's great, too.

5. Once you have a strategy, set up your accounts and begin uploading photos. Set a daily or weekly goal for yourself: something like five photos a day or twenty-five photos a week.

6. As time goes on, learn what works and what doesn't. Microstock photography may not be the pathway to riches, but some people have been able to create a significant, ongoing revenue source after getting up and running.

START A SUBSCRIPTION SITE

Have you noticed that more and more businesses have switched to monthly or annual pricing? That's because they're smart—they want to get paid over and over, not just once. *You* can get paid over and over, just like those businesses, at least if you build a subscription service into your offer. The technical process of building a subscription site (also known as a membership site, and sometimes by some other terms) is easy enough. The hard work lies in acquiring and retaining customers.

BUSINESS MODEL: Establish sustainable, predictable income through a subscription service.

WHY: People are used to paying for monthly services, and they'll pay for them for a long time *if* you can create something valuable enough.

AVERAGE STARTUP COST: Variable.

EASE OF STARTUP: Low.

LONG-TERM POTENTIAL: High.

SKILLS REQUIRED: Basic technical ability, human relations, and the knowledge of something specific that makes your subscription site stand out.

BENEFITS: Sustainable, predictable income!

DOWNSIDES: Potential to get bored with the hustle while you still have active members; some resistance to membership models from people who don't want to pay more than once.

WORKFLOW:

1. First and foremost, get clear and specific on your service. What can you offer people that will be useful over and over?
2. Select a platform to manage subscriptions. You'll need to make sure you (a) consistently deliver new content or ongoing access to the service, and (b) collect payments on time.
3. Create the introductory materials and onboarding process for your subscription site.
4. Consider a free trial (or low-cost trial) membership to get prospects in the door.
5. Tell the world!
6. Do everything you can to deliver an *amazing* service to people once they sign up. First impressions matter a lot: if they stick around for a few months, chances are they'll remain indefinitely.

How to Validate an Idea with $10 and a Facebook Account*

Do you have $10? Have you ever used Facebook? I'm guessing the odds are 99 percent or higher that the answer to both questions is yes. If you have a big idea and want to get some real-world feedback (not just from your friends) before going further, you can simply set up an advertisement and see how people respond. No need to rent a billboard—with Facebook you can get it going in less than an hour and as little as $10.

Here's how.

1. Write a blog post or create a short video all about the problem that your new hustle will solve. Go deep: describe how the problem seriously affects people's lives, and paint the picture of what life would be like if that problem were solved. At the very end, mention the potential solution (your idea!), and include a link to a landing page where people can sign up to learn more.

2. Create a Facebook page dedicated to your potential hustle. Post three to five links, images, or videos related

___

* To compile this exercise, I relied on notes from Claire Pelletreau, an expert on Facebook advertising. Completing the analysis takes an hour or so to implement, but for a lot of hustles, it's worth it. Get more info from Claire, including detailed screenshots of how to set it up, at SideHustleSchool.com/claire.

to the problem you solve before running any ads. This is so that when someone sees your ad and clicks on the name of the page, they don't see a completely deserted Facebook page.

3. Define your first "audience" for the ad. This is Facebook's term for the people who will see your ad. When you go through the interface, you'll be asked a series of questions to narrow down the audience. For this exercise, your audience should have no more than 50,000 people in it.

4. Use different interests or demographics to map out a second audience. This is so you can show your ad to two distinct groups of people to see if either responds better. For example, you may want to test men versus women, married people versus single people, people who "like" show tunes versus those who "like" hip-hop, or any number of other variables.

5. Write some strong copy for your ad. When in doubt, make it long—short ad copy is often too vague or boring. You could even use the first couple of paragraphs of your blog post as your ad text.

6. Find a great image for your ad. This is important, because people will be drawn to strong visual images. You can find plenty of free stock photography online (just be sure it's really free—if you're not sure, it probably isn't). Unsplash.com is one source that I've used before.

7. Post your blog post to your Facebook page, using your ad copy above the link. If the image Facebook pulls from

your post is different from the one you wanted, it's easy to change it.

8. "Boost" your post, selecting the audience that you put together in step #3. Spend $5 and have the boosted post run for forty-eight hours.

9. "Boost" the same post again, this time with the second audience you selected. Spend $5 again and let it run for forty-eight hours.

10. After you've spent the $10, take a look at your metrics. How many clicks did your ad get, and which audience responded better? How many people clicked on the link to your landing page? How many actually signed up?

If 10 percent or more of the people who landed on your blog post clicked on the link to your landing page, that's widely considered to be a pretty good sign that people are interested in the product or service that you're thinking of offering.

APPENDIX 3
Write a Letter to Your Ideal Customer

When John Lee Dumas wrote thirteen hundred words about Jimmy, his ideal podcast listener, he gained a clear understanding of the people he wanted to serve. The description even included the names and ages of Jimmy's imaginary children, how he liked to exercise, and what he watched on TV when he came home from work!

You may not need to get *that* detailed, but don't skip the most important part: understanding the pain that your ideal customer (also known as an avatar) is going through. In Jimmy's case, that pain was his day job. Every day he spent hours trapped in the cubicle, not finding any meaning in the work but having to do it anyway to support his family.

If you're having trouble understanding your avatar on this deep a level, it may help to write them an actual letter, focusing on who they are and what you're able to do to help them.

Imagine that your side hustle is selling fans—really big, powerful ones. Ultimately, the people who need your fans are workers in a warehouse, but those aren't the people who make the purchasing decisions. Therefore, you decide that your avatar is the manager or owner of a small-but-growing manufacturing business that is located in an especially warm climate. Here's what you might say to this person:

Hey there,

You have a growing business, and sales are hopping. To keep up with demand, you've had to hire more people. Your warehouse is a big space, so it's hard to keep cool, and air-conditioning isn't an option. Throughout the day, you notice that your employees work hard, but inevitably they get tired and run-down in the heat. That's no surprise: it's really hot! Those off-the-shelf fans won't cut it.

I know what it's like—back when I was in college, I used to work in a warehouse. Most employees didn't last very long in the summer, even when they were hard workers.

That's why, after I grew up and took another job, I spent all my free time designing the world's best ceiling fans. These fans aren't cheap, but when you install them, you'll see an immediate difference.

From the very first day you install my fans, your employees will be happier and healthier. Your business will end up retaining them longer and making more money. Most of all, you'll be able to focus on growing the business, and you won't have this nagging heat problem any more.

Can I help? Sincerely,

The Fan Guy

Notice a few key elements of the letter:

I know who you are. I'm not just a random person. I've taken the time to appreciate your unique situation.

I feel your pain. I've been there! I used to work in this environment, so I understand the challenge.

I have the solution. After countless hours of research, I've developed a much better fan than everything else out there.

The solution is worth it. I'm not selling the cheapest fans, but your investment will pay off.

Consider writing a letter like this to your ideal customer. Talk to them directly and show that you understand their needs. Propose a solution and build a relationship with this imaginary person. The more you know who they are—and of course, how you can help them—the easier it will be to turn them from an imaginary customer into a real one.

APPENDIX 4
Buy a Rental Property with a $1,575 Down Payment

In the prehistoric days of side hustling, most of what you heard about "multiple streams of income" related to real estate, specifically the idea of buying multiple properties and renting them out. I haven't written about that in this book at all, partly because it's been well covered elsewhere but also because I don't know much about it.

Fortunately, I have a friend and industry expert whom I refer people to for advice whenever they ask. This friend and expert, Paula Pant, publishes a blog called AffordAnything.com, where she chronicles her adventures in real estate investing. In a series of detailed posts, she publishes her full income and expenses report for each property every month.

I've been a longtime fan and reader, but I've also wondered how replicable her approach was for average people who don't have a lot of savings. Isn't it much too difficult and expensive for most people to get into real estate investing? Plus, isn't the industry a bit over-hyped and intimidating?

Thus began an email exchange between me and Paula, where I asked her to shed light on these questions and explain her unconventional approach. An abbreviated version, complete with tips from Paula, is below.

Q. How does this work? My perception is that real estate investing isn't a great starter business or side hustle.

A. Owning rental properties is like traveling: most people assume it's expensive, but the truth is that it can cost much less than you think. If this is something you truly want to pursue, you can make it happen.

Let's move past platitudes and examine real numbers. First, let's start with the fact that you don't need to own property in your backyard. Invest where you'll get great returns; go where the money is. I live two thousand miles away from my rentals.

Across many parts of the United States and Canada, you can find great rental properties selling for around $50,000 to $100,000. My most recent home purchase is a four-bedroom, two-and-a-half-bathroom brick ranch in Atlanta that I bought for $46,000, as a short sale. Just now I spent two minutes looking online and found a single-family home in the neighborhood where I grew up. It's currently listed for $45,000, also as a short sale.

If you live in an area that features low-priced homes, you can apply for an FHA loan, which only requires a 3.5 percent down payment. On a $45,000 home, that's a down payment of just $1,575. I'd recommend having another $2,000–$3,000 in your bank account to deal with any emergencies that arise. That's not as cheap as a $100 startup, but it's far less than people think.

Finally, don't assume that banks and credit unions are the only source of mortgage loans. Many private lenders offer loans with zero money down. We used a private lender to buy House #3, and although we pay a higher interest rate—ours is 7 percent—we also collect about $3,000 per year in passive income from that house, with nothing out of pocket.

Q. Okay, so is it all about buying far away from home? If I live in California, should I really buy a house in Detroit?
A. That's silly. If you live in San Francisco, why would your brain immediately make the leap to Detroit? Reno is approximately three hours away. You can drive there on Saturday morning, spend the afternoon, and return back home in time to hit the bars on Saturday night.

This is true for any major city. Seattle is a couple hours from Port Angeles. Portland is a few hours from Boise. L.A. is four hours from Vegas. Manhattan is a couple hours from Philadelphia.

Besides, you won't need to make many trips. One to see the home after you're under contract. If everything runs smoothly and if you don't buy a fixer-upper, that's the only trip you'll need to make. If you buy something in need of repair, you'll need to make a few more trips to check on the contractors' work. And that's about it. Your property manager and contractors will handle everything else.

Q. Great. What should I do next?
A. Here are my top three tips:

1. Don't assume you need to buy an investment property in your own backyard. Go where the money is.
2. Buy for the sake of cash flow, instead of speculating about potential future home value. I like to say that "appreciation is speculation." You can't control the market. Focus within your circle of control, and pick a property that creates great cash flow.
3. If you decide to handle any of the work yourself, such as property management or renovations, run your preoffer analysis as though you're *not* going to. This way, you can remove yourself from those responsibilities, hire someone else at fair market rates, and your returns stay the same.

Page for People Who Read the Notes at the End

Common sense is not always common. When I first presented the five-week plan to my editor, it was a four-week plan. "Do you think it might be good to add some steps about how to actually implement an idea?" she asked. What a concept! (Thank you, Talia.)

After some discussion it was decided that "Test, Test, and Test Again" would be a better phrase for the chapter on testing than "The booty doesn't lie." The author resisted, pointing out the merits of referencing popular culture, as well as the benefit of providing a shoutout to anyone who identifies with or merely appreciates the word *booty*, but was defeated.

Not every side hustle made the cut for the final manuscript draft. Regretfully, a story of someone who ships live crickets to reptile owners was removed after much editing. Also eliminated from consideration: non-alcoholic Jell-O shots, a kit to prevent seagulls from nesting on roofs (slogan: "Seagull proof your roof!"), and an alarm clock that electrocutes your nipples.

It is no exaggeration to say that I write for the Most Awesome Readers in the Universe. I loved writing this book, but I'm even more excited to see what you do with the ideas and instruction. Here's to your hustle!

To be continued . . .

Resources and Free Stuff

I get a lot of requests for specific tools and resources. I've mentioned some of them in the book, but there are others—and sometimes the specific recommendations change as time goes by. For the most updated list, please visit **SideHustleSchool.com/resources**. There you'll find:

- How to build your first website in 90 minutes

- Where to host that website for less than $5 a month

- A thirty-day free trial of an email list management service to help you build an audience

- A twenty-one-day free trial of Shopify (great for selling physical products)

- A free audiobook copy of *Born for This*, my last book (available with a trial membership from Audible)

- A free pony*

---

* Note: Pony may not be available in all markets. But there might be some other things! I want to make sure you feel fully supported in your hustling adventures.

Index

ABOUT THE AUTHOR

CHRIS GUILLEBEAU is the author of the *New York Times,* *Wall Street Journal,* and *USA Today* bestseller *The $100 Startup* and the *Wall Street Journal* bestsellers *The Happiness of Pursuit* and *Born for This.* His blog receives more than one million unique hits a month, and posts have been picked up everywhere from CNN.com to Forbes .com to the *Huffington Post.* His newsletter is read by more than 80,000 subscribers, and he is the creator and emcee of the World Domination Summit, an annual gathering of cultural creatives. Over the course of a lifetime of self-employment and side hustling, he visited every country in the world (193 in total) before his thirty-fifth birthday.

DISCOVER THE LIFE YOU WERE BORN TO LEAD WITH OTHER BESTSELLERS FROM CHRIS GUILLEBEAU!

"*The $100 Startup* is a twofer: It's a kick in the pants to get started on your dream and a road map for finding your way once you begin. **If you're not ready to launch your own business after reading this book, you need to go back and read it again!**"

—Daniel H. Pink, *New York Times* bestselling author of *Drive* and *A Whole New Mind*

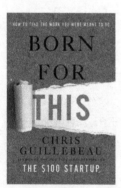

"Intensely practical and packed with real-life examples, *Born for This* is the essential guide for a career that will bring you not just a paycheck but true happiness."

—Gretchen Rubin, *New York Times* bestselling author of *The Happiness Project* and *Better Than Before*

CHECK THEM OUT AT
CHRISGUILLEBEAU.COM/BOOKS/

CROWN
BUSINESS
NEW YORK